FEEL THE LAUGHTER
Sharon Patyk Komlos

FEEL THE LAUGHTER
Sharon Patyk Komlos

Trillium Press
New York

Trillium Press, Inc.
PO Box 209
Monroe, New York 10950
(914) 783-2999

Printed in the United States of America
ISBN: 0-89824-150-2

Dedication

This book is dedicated with love to my parents,
   Richard and Florence Patyk
to my loving and most remarkable children,
   Shawn, Marc, and Kristin
and especially to the man I deeply love and admire,
   Raymond D'Eusanio

Acknowledgements

I would like to acknowledge and express my sincerest thanks to the people who have touched my life in a very special way. These are the people who came into my life after the incident which sparked the writing of this book. I have never seen them with my eyes, but have felt their sincerity, love and compassion.

Charles Greenwood, the man who was not afraid to get involved and came to my rescue.

That very special nameless individual who sent me the court transcripts at no cost to the victim.

Ralph and Alice McNeely, for saving me from myself and transcribing my tapes for this book.

Ferne Robin, of PIP printing for her "on the spot" copying of my original manuscript.

To the people who helped me to get started in bringing my story to the public from the podium.

Dr. Wayne Dyer, for introducing me to the speaking profession.

Allen Cushman, June Aiken and the entire Board of Directors of Crime Stoppers of Palm Beach County.

Sgt. Bob Price, Sgt. Dan Crist, Lt. Jerry Poreba and members of the Crime Prevention Officers of Palm Beach County.

H. Coleman Tily and the entire Board and staff of Crime Stoppers International.

Karen M. Leach, for introducing me to the high school audience and her ongoing friendship.

I would especially like to acknowledge a person who came into my life when I could still see: Charles Lore, for his love and support and for his unconditional and continuous friendship.

I am also most grateful to the entire staff at Trillium Press, especially to Myrna Kay for being so understanding and patient. Most of all I would like to thank Dr. Thomas M. Kemnitz who truly believes in me and this project.

This book would have never reached the hands of my publisher if it were not for the love and dedication of one very special individual. These acknowledgements would not be complete without recognizing Raymond D'Eusanio, who was my eyes. My deepest gratitude is given to him for always being here.

Halloween

The worst point in my life came when I waited alone in the dark in fear. I suppose that all of us have known such moments. What made mine different was that both the darkness and the fear were man made, and I was not allowed in a courtroom where a crucial decision to me was being made by people who were not even considering me. I was afraid because I had no control over the situation, and no defense if they made the wrong decision.

The darkness was for life—an act of malevolence. One night in May while I was driving on the highway, a man in another car had shot me. The bullet took my sight. The man then kidnapped me, stabbed me, attempted to suffocate me, raped me, and left me for dead. Through it all, I had planned and struggled to survive and to minimize the damage.

The planning and struggling had continued for another five months. The man had been caught. I had been safe with my family. Now it seemed that it might start over again.

My attacker was standing trial. He was pleading insanity. There was the very real possibility that he might soon again be out on the roads. Would I have to deal with this evil menace another time? I had heard for years about the "criminal justice system" in the United States. Now I was a victim of it. It was the source of my fear. It might be protecting the rights of my attacker, but it had failed to protect me. And now it was not letting me live in peace.

In the name of "criminal justice," I had to testify in court, but I was not allowed to hear any of the rest of the trial. There was some concern that it might prejudice the rights of the defendant if the jury had to see every day the woman he had rendered blind for life. So I was brought in and led out—and left alone to deal with my blindness and the possibility that this evil man might some day be free to inflict injury again on me, on my little daughter, on any one he cared to aim his gun at. His right to a fair trial, mine to blindness and terror: Our criminal justice system at work.

How had all this happened? Would it ever end? How could I take control of my life again? Would I ever again be the happy mother of three, aspiring career woman, and contented wife I had been on May 22, 1980?

CHAPTER ONE

May Day

I worked a full day on May 22nd at my job as an Insurance Claims Adjuster. I picked up my three children at their day care center, took them home, fixed them dinner, got them ready for bed, and left them with a baby sitter. I had family obligations—my brother's girl friend was in town. My husband did not want to accompany us, so I played tour-leader on my own.

After the tour, I went straight for home, exhausted by my full day. I was within ten minutes of our house on a road I took every day to and from work. There was another car just behind me—a dark Maverick with only one working headlight. As the car pulled alongside of mine, I kept my attention and eyes fixed on the road in front of me. Suddenly, there was the loud noise of a shot and I saw a bright flash of light—the last thing I would ever see.

I knew right away that I had been shot and that I could not see. I had to stop my car before I crashed into something. The impact of the bullet knocked me to the right. I managed to keep my hands on the steering wheel and moved my foot from the gas to the brake. I knew the road surface. I had already cleared the bridge over the turnpike, and there was nothing but the soft shoulder off the road to my left. I did not want to take a chance on the left shoulder because I knew that I had to cross over one lane of traffic before I would come to the wide median that separated the east and west lanes. I was not sure just how far I could pull off the road to the right before I would hit the trees or come to a canal. I was able to sit upright again and turned the wheel to the right. I applied pressure to the brake and heard the tire noise change when I pulled over. The car finally came to a complete stop. I was relieved that I managed to stop the car safely; after all it was new, my husband prized it, and I did not want to be the first one to put a dent in it.

I reached down for the lever to put the car into park. I knew that I needed help immediately. Somehow I had to draw someone's attention.

I tried to find the electric lever to raise my window. I was afraid that the person who had shot me might come back, and I wanted to be sure that the window was all the way up. The doors were already locked. As I felt around in the darkness trying to find the lever for the window with my left hand, I reached for the horn with my right. I intended to lay on the horn until I received help. I had not even assessed my injury with my hands. I knew it must be serious because everything was totally black. I had difficulty breathing. I could not tell if it was the result of mucus or blood. I felt the warm sensation of blood running down my face. I did not bother to turn off the ignition. I totally forgot about the lights to the car, and I left them on as well. I forgot to turn on the emergency flashers. I could not see anything to remind me to give visual signs of distress.

I found the lever for the window, finally. I thought I could feel safe until help arrived. I started to push upward, but my finger slipped off. As I pushed on the horn I felt an arm reach in the window, and I heard a man's voice. A man's hand pushed me back, and my hand fell from the steering wheel. The voice spoke out of the darkness, "My God, who did this to you?" The tone was one of shock and concern.

"I think that I have been shot. I can't see a thing. I need to get to the hospital," I said. The man opened my car door and helped me out. My car was left at the side of the road. I left the lights on, the ignition running, and my purse on the seat. None of these things seemed to matter. All I cared about was getting to the hospital.

The man lifted me over his shoulder to get me to his car quicker. He opened the driver's side door and pushed up the seat. He laid me gently on the floor of the back seat. It was a small car with an equally small rear seat. He made me as comfortable as he could under the circumstances. I rested my head gently on the rear seat. My body could handle the hard rear floor, but my battered head needed the cushion of the back seat. Now I had time to feel my wound. My eyes were shut and were already very much swollen to the touch, but there was no pain. I flashed back to the moment of impact; there was no pain then either. *"Am I in shock?"* I asked myself. My hands were now wet and sticky with blood which covered my face and hair. *"I must look an absolute mess. Thank God I can still think."* The man in the front seat began to speak in a nervous tone.

"I am fairly new in this area, and I do not know my way around too good. Is there a hospital close by that you would like to go to?"

I remembered how the children's emergencies had acquainted me with the local hospitals when I had first moved to the area. I knew that I did not want to go where I had taken them. I had been told that Holy Cross Hospital had one of the best emergency rooms in the area, and I thought that even if it was a little farther it would be well worth the extra time to get the much better care. I spoke out of my thoughts, "Holy Cross. Turn around and head back the other way. You want to go east until you hit Federal Highway." I thought that would be the easiest way to go for a person new in town. I could have told him to take the Interstate, but I was afraid that he would miss the exit. Since this was an emergency, I knew that red lights would not pose a problem. He could make it there in no time. "The hospital will be on the right on Federal. Let me know when you get to Federal Highway, it may have the sign that just says US1." I added that I used to live around this area and that if he thought that he was getting lost, he should tell me what he could see so I could guide him.

I was talking and thinking logically, *"Am I in shock?"* I kept asking myself. I had seen people in shock before and they appeared irrational. I thought I was being very rational. I felt the motion of the car and heard the passing of other cars. I slipped into thought. *"Here I am, shot in the head, unable to see a thing, and the rest of the world does not even know about it. People in all these cars going by do not even realize that I am in the back seat lying on the floor covered in blood."* Instantly the words, *"shot in the head,"* came to the foreground of my mind. I always thought that being shot in the head was associated with brain damage. What if this was my case? I already knew that I could still think. I knew that I could move my left and right hands. I was able to stand up, but I could not remember if I could feel my feet. The man had snatched me up so quickly, that I did not recall really feeling them. I tried wiggling my toes inside my shoes. I still had feeling. The best that I could tell I had no brain damage, but I could not see, and I had the intuition that I never would again. I was usually right with my intuitions. I remembered how I knew I was pregnant before the doctor did with all three of my children. I always had a feeling in the pit of my stomach when I knew what an outcome was going to be. I had the same feeling now. I already knew the outcome of this condition.

My thoughts were interrupted by the man's voice. It was not directed at me, but I overheard the mumbling, "Wouldn't you know it, a red light."

I decided to speak up, "That is exactly what you want, go through them, this is an emergency, if the police should stop you they can help." I could feel myself getting excited. I started to raise my head off of the back seat.

The man sensed what I was trying to do. "Please," he said firmly, "keep your head down, you will start to bleed too much, I was a medic in the service. Please, just talk calmly, and try to relax, try not to lose consciousness."

I did feel a bit dizzy when I tried to get up. I knew the man was right. "My name is Sharon Komlos, let me give you all my information right now before we get to the hospital, just in case I pass out."

"Talk slowly," he once again reminded me, "just keep down and try to relax."

I told that man I had three children, I told him their names and ages. I asked him to have the hospital call home for me so that they would not worry. "What kind of car is this?" I thought this was a rather stupid question to ask him, but I did not know what else to say, and I felt that I had to keep the conversation going because I was starting to feel faint.

"Why do you ask?

"I am an insurance adjuster, and I spend quite a bit of time looking at cars. I know it feels small and it is an older model. I just want to see if I am right."

The man answered in a calm voice just as though it were a normal course of an every day conversation having a little chat with a woman in the back seat of his car. "I really do not know. It is not mine. I think it is a 1970 or 1971 Maverick or something like that."

My end of the conversation had once again turned to the children. Then I reinforced the importance of telling the nurses to call home for me. I told him how I had moved to Florida only a year ago and that I really liked it. You could not beat the winters. He told me that he was new in town and was from the North also. I had no difficulty detecting his New York accent. "Why did you stop again?" I asked.

"There is a drawbridge, always when you are in a hurry. Wouldn't you know it." His voice was impatient, and why shouldn't it be?

Wait a minute, I thought. "You are going the wrong way, there is no drawbridge the way that you should be going. You made the wrong turn. You should have gone straight on Federal Highway. You must have made a left turn onto Fourteenth instead. Turn around and go back west until you pick up Federal again." Again I was getting excited.

"Oh yeah, I guess I was not paying attention."

I decided to keep still, I could feel the blood still flowing every time I tried to get up or got excited. "I think I'll lie quietly," I told him. There was no response from the front seat. I knew he was now concentrating more on where he was going. I felt some rail road tracks and knew that there were none near Holy Cross. I did not correct him this time because I knew that he must have passed up Federal again but if he was past the tracks he would soon be coming to North Ridge Hospital. That would be just fine with me. At least I would be somewhere. Again I spoke to my savior. "Just in case we get there and I do not get a chance to talk with you again I want to tell you how much I appreciate your help. I could have died if you did not stop to help me. I want to say thank you right now, at least I know I will eventually get home to my children." He remained silent. I thought to myself, *"And people say that others are reluctant to get involved. How wonderful it is that there are still some people who care about their fellow human beings and take the time to help. This man is new in town and went out of this way to help me when he saw that I was unable to help myself."* I felt relieved.

"We are almost there," he said, "It won't be long now."

Those were the magic words. I started to concentrate on just what I was going to tell the nurses and the doctors. At this point I did not feel that I would be unconscious when we arrived. I myself could give them all the information needed. I wondered where the bullet came from. I knew it was from the lone car that was passing me on the left, but I wondered why any one wanted to shoot me. I had begun asking myself questions that I knew the police ask. I was positive that the police would be called in immediately. I could not help wondering if I was just another random victim or some spin-off from the Miami riots in Overtown. They had ended only a few days earlier. I remembered reading in the newspaper how some people had been shot in the streets by rioters with no particular target in mind. Was I just one more? All I remembered was the flash and then the pop and then the darkness. The road just disappeared.

I had everything in order in my mind. I would give my name, address, and phone number. I would tell them to contact home for me and my husband, Wayne, not to worry, that I was all right. I would fill him in on the details when I got home. There was no use in worrying the children when I was not there to show them I was all right. I chuckled to myself when I thought about no brain damage. Some of the body shop men thought that I had nothing there to damage in the first place. They would joke in their own gruff ways with the cliché about dumb blonds and would be quick to qualify their comments when I gave them my look that said, "We'll see who is so dumb when you are working from my estimate." If they could see me now what would they think of the woman who hated to get grease on her skirt and could not stand to have her hair or makeup a mess? I was glad in an odd sort of way that

I could not see myself at that moment.

Of course if I could see myself, I would not be on my way to the hospital right now. The pessimist in me whispered that I would never see again. It was just too dark, and it felt so final. The optimist in me said that it was just the trauma of the bullet, and I was not positive that it was a bullet. That I was injured by a bullet was only an assumption. The realist in me argued that the flash of light had to come from something which more then likely was a gun. The darkness could very well be a permanent thing, but somehow I would be all right. Modern medicine was making great strides and permanent loss of sight might well be rectified by some sort of futuristic eye. "What would it be like to be blind?" I wondered.

I was not sure how much time had passed, but it seemed like fifteen or twenty minutes. I gave up on telling the man to go through red lights, I guess he just wanted to get us to the hospital in one piece. He probably had his reasons for not wanting to be stopped by the police, maybe he was just afraid of them as some people are. I used to be intimidated by the uniform when I was younger, and I remembered how some parents often used the police as a method of discipline. If you are not good, I'll call the police, and they will come and put you in jail. I did not use this with my children. I knew that someday they might need the help of the police. I did not want them to be afraid to ask for it. I knew that the man was being cautious to obey all the traffic rules. He was courteous and seemed to be nice. So what if he did not go through the red lights. That did not make him a criminal, just a safe driver.

His little Maverick came to a halt. "Well, here we are."

I began to speak quickly once again. "Please go inside and tell them that I was shot in the head and that I cannot see. Tell them that I am going to need a stretcher. Get the nurse and tell her to call the police for help . . ." I heard the car door open on the driver's side.

"You wait here for a second. Let me go in first to see if I can find out if I am in the right place. Just be quiet and stay calm. Rest for a second while I go inside. I will be right back." The car door slammed, and I could hear the footsteps leaving. I did not hear the normal noises that you would hear at a hospital, but I knew that it must be late. The hospital I thought we had reached is not very big, and it was more than likely a slow night. After all it was a weeknight, not the busy weekend that one would expect in Ft. Lauderdale. Hospital zones are usually quiet, except for the sound made by the ambulances. I had arrived in a Maverick, not an ambulance. All was quiet. I felt my head once again. "What a mess,"

I uttered out loud. My hair was wet and in some parts even sticky. I could smell the dried blood on my hands. I was surprised that I could smell anything the way that my nose felt. Maybe it was the blood inside my nose that I could smell. How awful! I did not feel odd talking to myself, there was no one to hear me.

I heard the footsteps in the distance coming closer. He first walked over to the passenger side of the car. Maybe he had forgotten that he has placed his passenger in the back on the floor so she could rest easier. The footsteps moved behind the car then over to the driver's door. There was a slight pause before he opened the door. I was beginning to get impatient and started to get up. The door opened. "They did not have any stretchers available. They said that there was a real bad crash on the I-95 Interstate and all of the emergency patients were brought here. They only have a small staff on hand here late at night, they asked if it would be possible for you to walk and come inside. I told them that I would check with you. Do you think that you can walk? I can help you."

I was anxious to get into the emergency room. I really did not need a stretcher. I thought I could walk, that was not the injury. "Yes, I can walk. I may need a little help getting out of the car though. Let me get up slowly." He pushed the front seat forward. I was able to stretch my cramped legs from the position they had been folded in underneath me. I held my head up at first by supporting it with my hands. "Boy, am I going to have a headache in the morning," I said out loud.

"Don't worry," he said, "it will be well taken care of." His voice was still calm and soothing. He helped me peel myself off the floor of the back seat. I felt a little dizzy when I stood up, and I had to lean on him for support. "Just take it slow," he reinforced. We just stood there for a second. "Are you alright now?"

I forgot and tried to nod my head. *"That was not very bright,"* I thought. It was just old instinctive reaction taking over.

"Yes, I think I'm OK to go in now."

He put one arm around my waist and I put my hands out to feel the way. He held and steadied me with both of his strong hands. He walked fast. We came to a flight of concrete steps, I figured that they must have had a ramp for the stretchers and the wheelchairs. There was a steel railing that I was able to hold on to. I thought we must have been a real sight. I was afraid that I might scare the hospital personnel when they saw me. At least they knew that I was coming. I hoped that they were ready for what I looked like. "Wait a second while I get the door for you." He opened the door and we went inside. I felt the man's arms and hands nudge me inside. The door closed behind us. I heard the door being locked. With that sound, my feelings of security in the company of my savior changed. In a split second, I felt his hands shove me down on a mattress. He was no longer concerned about my dizziness, or that I just might loose consciousness. He did not care if I started to bleed again or not. I tried to get up. He shoved me back down again.

I screamed for the very first time, "This is not a hospital, my God, where am I?" I felt a pillow come down over my face to stifle any further screams. I felt myself starting to faint. I felt his weight on the pillow. I could not see him, and now I could not breathe. I started to go limp and all the noises began to fade. *He is trying to kill me! My God, he is really trying to kill me!*

I could feel the pillow pressing harder and harder against my face. It was very important for me to breathe, and I did not like the idea of someone cutting off my air. I knew I had to do something quickly or I might never draw a free breath again. Everything that I had heard about self defense went down the drain. The most common suggestion that I remembered was to try to aim for the most vulnerable part of the male body. I could not find that tender area. As I struggled to free myself from the confines of the pillow, I also tried to raise up my knee in the hope he would somehow fall into it. This did not work. He had a three-fold advantage: he was bigger, he was stronger, and he could see. I had no weapons, and my purse had been left in my car. I kept struggling, picking up a scant amount of air every now and then, just enough to keep going. I had on high heels, and I tried to get one off of my foot. I managed to loosen the strap around my ankle just enough to slip off my shoe. I reached down with my right hand and grasped the shoe firmly. I started to hit in the area where I thought his head was. The heels were hard, and I hoped that I might be able to knock him unconscious.

I kept on hitting him and knew that I was doing some damage because his energy now concentrated on trying to get the shoe out of my hand rather than trying to suffocate me with the pillow.

I kept striking out, not caring where I hit him just as long as I made some sort of contact. I had forgotten about my head wound and became concerned only with saving my life. He pulled the shoe out of my right hand and threw it across the room. I heard it hit the wall then the floor. I started for the left shoe, but he got there first. As he concentrated on unbuckling the left ankle strap, I got a good hold on the pillow and pushed it away from my face. "Hey, wait a minute!" I screamed.

He stopped everything. "What's the matter?" he asked in calm voice, as if nothing had been going on.

"You are suffocating me, I can't breathe."

"Oh, I'm sorry," he apologized.

I just lay there for a moment; I could not believe what I had just heard. He apologized for almost suffocating me. He knew that he was doing something wrong. Why was he doing it in the first place? I could not understand what was going on. All of a sudden the course of events made sense. *"The small car behind me could have been a Maverick. The sound of the car as it started to overtake me was in fact the same sound of the car in which I was riding. Why didn't I think of this sooner? I was thankful someone had stopped for me, that was why. I had faith in human nature, but in this case I was wrong. Would it cost me my life?"* It was quiet in the apartment. What was going on I wondered? I heard the television go on, the TV was at my head, as I was lying sideways on the mattress. I heard him change the channel from somewhere at my feet. I knew that he had a remote control device. The television was kept low enough not to disturb the other tenants in the apartment but loud enough for him to hear. I felt his hands and his body moving towards me once again. I knew that the more aggressive I was with him the more aggressive he was with me. When I asked him what he was doing and told him that I could not breathe, he seemed to be a bit more calm. I heard noises that I associated with a medicine kit, like a doctor's black bag, back in the days when doctors made house calls. I remembered that he said that he was a medic in the service, did he have one of those black medical kits? I suddenly felt a pressure to my chest. I felt like he had injected me with something. I started to feel dizzy. I thought I was going to pass out.

I laid there quietly again, I felt his body over mine touching me. I felt more and more pressure to my arms the side of my neck and to my legs. I was too weak to fight back. I felt as though I were somewhere else. I listened to the television station. I heard the theme song for the *Twilight Zone*, I felt as though I had entered it. The bed became wet and sticky, I assumed that it was from my own blood. I started to get very cold. I heard the man walk around the room, he was pacing back and forth. His footsteps disappeared and then returned.

I could sense that he was not quite sure what he should do next. Was I correct in my assumption? Was he confused? What was he going to do with me next? It seemed better not to ask. The unknown was deadly scary, especially in the context of all the horror of the evening. What unknown cruel games could he play with me? My new darkness was frightening enough, what more could he do? I could hear the sounds of the man's voice mumbling to himself. I did not think he was speaking to me, and if he were I did not hear what he was saying and did not want to ask him to repeat himself. The television was still on, still low. I could hear the occasional passing of a car on the street below. I knew that it had to be early morning since there were so few sounds of movement. I heard him loosen his belt and unzip his pants. I heard his pants fall to the floor. I had the sick feeling in my stomach that I knew what was to follow. *"Why not?"* I started to get sarcastic with myself. *"It is only logical. First he shoots me to disable me and then comes back to pose as the good samaritan. Then he tries to suffocate me with the pillow, then the pressure to my chest and neck."* I raised my hand to the center of my chest where I had felt the puncture, there was what I assumed was blood because it was warm and wet. Was it a knife wound? I did not know for sure, and there was no one I could ask to confirm my suspicion.

I heard another soft sound. I guessed that it was his shirt. I felt cold and started to shiver. There was nothing I could use to cover myself. I felt so helpless lying there knowing that any movement might provoke him. I hated the feeling. I just waited. What else could I do? I felt his weight on the bed. He was ready to increase my misery. His hands reached around the front of my pants searching for the front zipper. He found it, unzipped it and pulled off my slacks. The panty hose and underpants were both pulled off in one quick motion. *"Should I fight back? Should I scream?"* I felt dizzy once again. He pulled my blouse off over my head without my assistance. I was still lying on the bed as he moved over me removing any clothing that he felt would hamper him from carrying out his next act of aggression. I was face down on the bed. He paused for just a moment and I could feel him position himself over my back. What else could he be up to but rape? I thought once again rape would be the logical course of events for his type of behavior. Rape is, after all, next to murder the ultimate expression of male violence. He forced himself in my anus, and I felt pain for the very first time that night. I felt as though he were ripping me apart. I wanted to cry out. Tears would not come to my swollen eyes. I kept telling myself it would be over soon, if I could only make it through this one more act of violence. I knew it had to end sometime, if I could only survive it. As I kept encouraging myself to stay alive, I tried to think about how I was going to save myself. Nothing came to mind. When the rape was over, the question became, "What next?" I did not know, nor did I care, if my attacker had climaxed. I wanted to ask him, "Why?" Why the shooting, the rape? Why did he do this to the mother of three small children? Did he have a mother of his own? Out of the black silence came the man's voice. "How was that, did you like it?"

"You have to be kidding. You cannot expect a reply." I did not intend to give him one. He asked again, and he sounded more anxious for some sort of answer. I decided it might be to my benefit to try to find out more about what this man wanted. Maybe I could use the knowledge. This was a stupid time for me to display pride, modesty, and rage. I had to use all my wits to survive.

"Did you enjoy it?" he asked again.

"Sure," was about all I could make myself say. "I'm cold," I said.

"Here, honey, let me help you." The man covered me with a comforter that was damp and cold itself. It felt heavy and did not ease my chill. "Are you okay, honey?" The man's voice had taken on a lighter, more endearing tone. This sounded more like the man in the car helping a women who had been injured. He called me by a name that I thought might have been that of some girl friend of his. He started talking inaudibly. He walked away from the bed, and I heard a door open.

He returned, speaking once again in a low voice. I heard the whine of a dog. He carried it into the room where I lay. *"What now?"* He sat down at the foot of the bed, with the dog in his arms. He was speaking to it gently. I listened to the man as he once again spoke to me, "Is that OK?" I did not know what he was referring to.

"How are the children?" I decided to turn the conversation, to remind him that I was a mother, to try to introduce some context beyond his torture chamber, and perhaps to change the rules of the game. My situation could only get worse if he succeeded in killing me, and anything was worth trying to make it better.

He seemed puzzled by my question. He replied anyway, "Oh, they are just fine . . . what children?"

Again I asked, "How is the baby?"

"The baby is fine, it is sleeping." Then he paused before I heard him mutter in a softer voice, "Do you have children? You are a mother."

Silence once again filled the room, except for the television which I could still hear in the background. The man once again sat down on the floor at the foot of the bed—never again getting on the bed with me. Every now and then I could feel his hand touch my feet, then my ankle. His hands came up to cover me as I shivered and then they would travel over to my breast. I could feel his eyes exploring his victim. I could feel him touching me, but I was unable to move. I was just too tired from my injuries, loss of blood, and lack of sleep. I felt his hand reach over to touch my wrist. He kept his hand there, just as a nurse does when taking a patient's pulse.

The violence had subsided, at least for the moment. I was exhausted. My mind was busy working out a way to free myself. I lost consciousness thinking about my children, wondering if I would ever be with them again. I knew that I had to be. I was determined to get out alive! I just had to work out the details.

I awoke in the early morning to the sound of the man snoring at the foot of the bed. *"Could this be my chance to make a break for it?"* Instead of acting hastily, I thought first. *"Where am I?"* I had no idea. I thought I knew where the telephone was, but I was not sure. *"Will I awake my attacker in searching for the phone? And if I should find it, will I be able to talk long enough for them to trace the call before he wakes up? Is he just pretending to be asleep?"* I did not know how soundly he was sleeping. *"If I should try to get out of here, where is the door to the outside? If I do get out, who will hear my screams and help me before the man wakes up?"* There was no traffic noise, and I could not be sure anyone would hear me. *"Just what are my chances right now?"* I assessed that they would not be good at all.

I asked myself one last, most important question. I had just gone through a very aggressive violent stage with this man. *"If I try to get out of the apartment and wake him up, will he awake in an aggressive state and really kill me or will he awake in a passive state?"* The risk was just too great. I decided to lie still and wait until morning when I would stand a better chance. I did not have the stamina to do otherwise.

I awoke to the sounds of the man moving around the apartment. I could tell that it was morning because of the street noises. I started to cough uncontrollably. Once again as so many times through the night I was shivering. I tried to pull the blood-soaked comforter tighter around me. I still could not control my coughing. I felt the congestion in my nasal passages and asked the man for a tissue. He brought me one small square of toilet tissue. This type of behavior was like that of a small child wanting to help and trying to but not exactly sure what was wanted of him. Then I asked him for a wet washcloth so I could wipe some of the blood and mucus from my face. This time he followed the instruction exactly as requested. I thanked him politely so I would not again, as the night before, invoke his violence.

I was very much frightened by even his seemingly kind behavior. For hours I had been held captive by this man, and I knew the horrors of which he was capable. I did not know if or when I would again be subjected to another attack by him. I kept thinking of how I was going to try to get help. My coughing had subsided, and I felt myself just go limp on the bed. I tried to tell myself that the whole thing would be over soon, that I would once again be home with the children, that they were still going to have a mother.

I heard his movement around the room and could not help wondering what he was doing. There was water running where I thought the bathroom was. The dog was once again put back into that room, and I assumed that the door was closed so it would not roam freely around the apartment. That dog was confined to its one room, and I was confined by my inability to see. *"How can I read the situation? How will I know when it is time to move? How will I know where to move?"* The television was still at the same volume.

I could hear a plastic being unfolded over me as I lay on the bed. I assumed it was a bag and wondered what its contents would be. I felt another chill. I coughed again, and then tried my best to be still and concentrate on his every move. I heard what sounded like gun shells being shaken from a gun and tossed into the trash bag. I felt the man remove the remains of my blouse from my left wrist, I did not realize that it was still clinging there. I heard the soft sounds of my clothing sliding into the bag. He removed my watch, then let my wrist fall limp to the bed. I heard the sound of car keys in his hands. All sounds except for those from the street ceased for a moment. I could picture him looking around the room for anything else that was mine. I heard his footsteps as he moved around the foot of the bed. *"Was I to be part of the trash?"* The television went silent for the first time. He walked away from me and then returned. I did not move. *"What now?"* I felt him staring at me. He picked up my right wrist, and held his fingers on my pulse. He kept them there for a few seconds, then let my arm fall to the bed. I lay limp and montionless with no sign of life. I could hear him turn away and leave a little faster and more confidently. I heard a door open and close. It sounded as though he locked it from the outside, or else he jiggled the handle to be sure that he had locked it from the inside.

It seemed too easy. *"Will he just leave me here? Does he know that I am still alive, or does he know something that I do not? When will he return? Did he just go outside to throw away that trash bag with my clothing and personal belongings and his shells?"* Then I heard the familiar sound of the engine of the car that attempted to pass me on

Sample Road. I could hear him put the car into gear. As the sounds faded into the distance, I knew my moment had come. There was no time to waste. I did not know if or when he would return. Acting as though I only had a few seconds to escape, I pushed myself off the bed, ignored my dizziness as I stood up, and concentrated on getting out. I knew my priority. First I tried to find a window because I really thought that he had locked the door from the outside. I trailed the walls all the way around the room following their outline with my hands. I felt a tight piece of material stretched over the wall, it was not a window I could get out. I felt heavy louvered doors over what I thought were the windows. I could feel the sun behind them. This would be too difficult. I decided to keep going. I let the traffic noises lead me to the door. I felt the handle and did not expect it to open, but, thank God, I was wrong. I had found the door to my freedom.

CHAPTER TWO

A Stitch in Time

As I stepped through the door, I entered a world of busy morning traffic noise. I felt concrete underfoot. *"Someone should be able to see me now."* But just in case I could not be seen, this "spectacle" was prepared to make a scene. I was going to let the whole world know exactly where I was. I took only a couple of steps forward because I was afraid of falling. I could feel the sunshine on my naked body. I had no time to be embarrassed. My life was at stake. I started to scream. I figured I could be heard all the way to Ohio. *"Why doesn't someone notice me?"* I started searching the small landing for something to throw over the edge. I found a fisherman's landing net. As I picked it up to heave it into the street, I heard a man's voice behind me. His voice was quick and sounded shocked.

"My God, who could have done this? I'll help you and take you to the hospital." Instantly I recalled those same words spoken to me by another man only the night before.

"Who are you?" I asked quickly.

"My name is Charlie. Don't you have any clothes? Who did this to you?" His voice was unfamiliar. I knew that he was not the same man. I also knew that I was not in a very good position. I needed medical treatment immediately, but I did my best in the circumstances to ensure that there would not be another samaritan like the previous night's.

"I think the man who did this took them with him, and I have no idea when he is going to return. Just hurry and get me out of here. There's no telling what he'll do to both of us if he should find us here. He's very dangerous."

I felt Charlie's hands on my waist guiding me towards those familiar concrete steps. He told me that he was on his way to work when he saw and heard me screaming on the balcony. He had his van from work and asked me if that was okay. I told him at this point that anything would be all right as long as I got to the hospital. He told me that he had a blanket and would give it to me as soon as I was inside the van.

I managed to climb up into the passenger seat. I heard Charlie's footsteps run around the back of the van. He started the engine quickly and pulled into the traffic, completely forgetting about the blanket. I tried to cover myself with my hands. I figured I would not slow him down by asking for a blanket. I did not want anything to interrupt this trip to the hospital.

Once again I gave the man instructions, "My name is Sharon Komlos. I live in Boca Raton. When we get to the hospital, please go inside and tell them that I need a stretcher. Tell them that I was shot in the head, and I am blind."

Charlie told me that he was going to take me to Broward General Hospital. It was the only one that he knew in the area, and we would be there in a few seconds. He told me just to stay calm and hold on. He admitted that he was nervous. I told him that I was, too.

I felt the van stop. As Charlie left the van, he yelled back to me just to stay there. I thought to myself, "*I have no other place to go.*" I reached down to feel what I thought was just a puncture wound in my chest. There was fresh, warm blood still oozing from the wound. I reached up and felt my hair. It was stiff and matted with dried blood. "*I must be a ghastly sight.*" I could hear Charlie's voice filled with urgency in the background. He was talking to another male voice. I could not tell what was being said, but I was sure that he was explaining what he had found. I sat there quietly, and the passenger side door opened. There were two unfamiliar soft women's voices.

"Do you need any assistance in getting down? We have a gurney here and some clean sheets. Come, I'll help you."

I felt a soft, gentle hand touch my elbow. It guided me gently out of the van and onto the ground. I then felt a clean sheet cover my body. Both of the women helped me up on the gurney and quickly wheeled me inside. "*I really made it,*" I thought. "*I'm here, finally. At last, someone cared enough to get involved. If it weren't for Charlie...*" I was unable to continue my thoughts. They were interrupted by the urgency of the doctor starting his examination and softly asking questions.

"Do you know where your injuries are? Can you direct me to them?"

As calmly as I could, I started to tell him, "I think I was shot. The left side of my head, right by the eye." I pointed to where I thought the injury was. "That is just the first wound. I felt a pressure in my chest and I think it is bleeding." I directed him to what I thought was the second. He started discussing the wounds with a nurse. He told her that it looked like a bullet wound. The left side of the temple was the entry point. He searched around to the right temple near my eye and found the exit point.

"Yes," he said, "there it is. The entry point and the exit point." He sounded relieved.

The nurse found another slice on my neck. The doctor and the nurse seemed to be more concerned with the chest wound. He wasn't sure exactly how deep it was, and his worry was that it might have punctured a lung. Fortunately, this was not the case. The knife had narrowly missed lung, aorta, and heart. The slash in the neck was strictly superficial—no danger there.

The doctor started giving his orders for an opthamologist, a neurosurgeon, and a cardiovascular surgeon. When I told him that I had been raped, he put in a call for the Rape Crisis Center.

I could feel a void to my left where the doctor had been standing. The nurse kept her position asking another to bring her some clean clothes and some water. Now they could get started.

The nurse started to clean away the dried blood.

"Look at this. There's blood even in your toes. You are literally covered from head to toe with dried blood."

"I can feel it. I feel absolutely filthy from the tip of my head all the way down my legs to my toes." She only confirmed my observations. I kept telling myself over and over, *"At least I'm safe, at least now I'll get the medical attention that I needed all night."*

As I lay there on the gurney in an emergency room, I tried to make some sort of sense of the noises and the voices that were surrounding me. That sense of urgency—people hustling to and fro. I spoke to the nurse cleansing my wounds. "I've been in many emergency rooms, usually with my children. Usually you take a number and wait, but you know, this is the very first time I was ever admitted to an emergency room and actually taken care of first."

The nurse did not laugh at my sense of humor, nor did she realize my sense of relief. I heard the voices in the background talking about x-rays, calling the police, contacting the Rape Crisis Center. I could pick up only bits and pieces in the conversations that I overheard. I was so busy listening and assessing my new surroundings that I had no time to reflect on what had just happened.

An unfamiliar voice joined those around the table. It was directed to the nurse cleansing my wounds. I could feel his cool hands on my forehead moving my stiff hair from the side of the entry wound, then working their way around to the exit area. The doctor lifted my eyelid and peered inside both eyes. I felt a sensation of warmth. I assumed it was from the bulb of the flashlight he was using to examine the insides and assess the damage. It felt odd not to be able to see that light.

"Can you tell me what happened, to the best of your recollection?" he asked.

"I think I was shot."

"Were you standing still?" he asked.

"No, I was driving my car. I was traveling about forty-five or fifty miles-an-hour and a car pulled up next to mine and I was shot. That's when I lost my sight."

"The police will be here soon. You can give them your story then," he said.

I sensed disbelief in his tone. I heard his footsteps leave. I really began to wonder if anybody would ever believe my story. I never thought that anybody would doubt it. *My God, where is the man who did this? Is he still out there somewhere on the loose? Who is he? Where did he come from? Why did he do this to me?"*

The nurse who was attending my wounds told me that I would be prepared for X-ray. The cardiovascular surgeon briefly looked at the chest wound. Apparently he thought it did not go deep enough to do serious damage. But X-rays would be needed just to be safe. I heard another strange voice speak to the young nurse. This doctor touched the bottom of my feet apparently looking for a reaction. I assumed he was the neurosurgeon. I talked to him briefly also telling him what had happened. I did not think that there was any brain damage, and once again I assumed that the reason for his examination was strictly a precautionary measure.

An unfamiliar woman's voice came from my right side. She identified herself as a representative of the Rape Crisis center.

"Sharon, is there anything at all I can do for you?"

I thought for a moment, "Do you know if anyone has contacted my husband yet?"

Before she left the room, she asked if I wanted to prosecute for the rape. It was very important to preserve the evidence properly so that it would be admissible in court. She explained the procedure. One of the doctors from the Rape Crisis Center would do the internal examination. She would stand by as a witness to document his findings. It was necessary to document his findings in order for the information to be admissible in court.

"Yes," I answered emphatically. "I did not realize that you needed my permission first. I just assumed..."

She broke in before I could continue. She told me that not all victims were willing to prosecute for a rape, that it was absolutely necessary to get my permission first before they could proceed. Once again I reiterated that I definitely wanted to prosecute for the rape. There was absolutely no doubt in my mind.

She thanked me for my cooperation and said that she would find out if my husband had been contacted. She said she would come back to let me know.

The footsteps continued in and out of the emergency room. Unfamiliar voices joined the familiar ones. The nurse who was still cleansing my body told me that I would be prepared for surgery in a little while, but first I would be taken to X-ray. I felt movement start. I could feel the movement of air over my body as I was wheeled down the corridor and into the X-ray room where I was told to lie still so X-rays could be taken of my head from different angles.

Immediately my left hand reached up into my hair. "What are you doing?" the nurse asked.

I kept searching with my fingers through my hair. "The night that I was shot I was wearing a ponytail on the left side of my head. It was fastened with a rubber band with a metal clasp. I know that will show up on the X-ray."

The nurse started to help me. "I really don't think anything is in there."

I kept on searching. "Here it is, look!" I started to tug at it and tried to pull it out but it was matted in the hair.

"Oh my gosh, look at that! That would show up in the X-ray!" the surprised nurse exclaimed. "Hold on a second. I'll be right back. I'm going to have to get some scissors to cut it out of there."

First the X-rays were taken of my head, next of my chest. I was then wheeled back to the emergency room. Once back inside, there were two unfamiliar voices; one a man's, the other a woman's. They identified themselves as detectives from the Fort Lauderdale Homicide Division.

"My name is Doug Haas, Sharon. I'll be investigating this case and this is my partner, Vicki Russo." He spoke to me in a soft, quiet, calming tone, telling me that everything was going to be all right, that they would be working the case, and that they would try their best to find the man. He told me that at a later date, when I felt like talking, they would need a statement from me telling them everything that had happened. But for now...

"I know how important these facts can be, and I know that the facts are going to start to fade with time." I continued by telling them I was an insurance adjuster and knew that people were poor witnesses at best, but at least now I still remembered some of the details of that night.

I heard Detective Haas ask quickly for a pencil and paper. "Okay, you can get started." I tried to give them every detail from the beginning of the evening. I started paying more attention to the details when I told them about the car following me and about the fact that there were no other cars on the road except for his and mine. I described the car as a dark-colored, small, Maverick-type car, older, with a loud engine. I told them it only had one working headlight. I told them how it started to overtake me on the left; how I kept my eyes straight ahead on the roadway and out of peripheral vision saw the flash of light, heard the popping sound, and the next thing I knew I was blind. I told them how I pulled the car off to the side of the road and how the good samaritan, so I thought, came up to offer assistance.

I told them about my ride to what I supposed to be the hospital, and how the man had taken me to his apartment. I told them detail-by-detail about the horrors of that evening. I described what I could remember of that apartment. I told them everything that I touched on my way out to safety. I told them about the tight piece of cloth pulled down over the window, about the heavy louvered doors, about the remote control for the television, and about the puppy. I gave them a description of what I thought to be the man's size, weight, and other physical characteristics. I told them about the plastic that he unfolded over me. I told them that I thought my clothing would be found in a plastic trashbag. I tried to given them every minute detail to assist them in apprehending the man.

As I spoke, I could hear the detective feverishly writing to take down every word that I said. Then I was silent.

"Is that all you can remember?" Detective Haas asked.

"I think so, at least that's all I remember right now. This whole thing just doesn't make sense," I said quietly. I was beginning to feel tired and my mouth was dry from talking. I was relieved that I had finally given all of the information to the police. Now it was up to them to find him.

The detectives told me that they would be back for a recorded statement later. For now, I had given them enough to start their investigation. They thanked me for my cooperation, and then said their good-byes. I thought that it was rather odd that they would thank me for my cooperation. Why wouldn't I help? I wanted my attacker off the streets just as much as they did.

Then a frightening thought filled my mind. Earlier that evening I had given him all of my home information. I told him where I lived and that I had three small children. I could not help worrying that my own family might be in danger. I could only hope that the police would find him, and find him very soon.

I heard the familiar voice of the young woman from the Rape Crisis Center. "I have checked around, and I found out that your husband was not contacted yet."

I asked her what time it was. She said it was twelve o'clock in the afternoon. *"My God, they must be frantic at home."* I gave the young woman my telephone number at home as well as Wayne's at work. I asked her to try both numbers to let him know where I was and that I was all right.

She also told me that the doctor from the Rape Crisis Center would arrive any minute and that after she made the phone call she would return with him to do the examination.

As she left the room I heard her say once more that she would be right back. I couldn't help wondering what was going on at home. Were my children in school? Did Wayne even know that I was missing? And what about work? Did they have any idea what had happened? I had told them yesterday that I would not be in until after lunch. Were they even aware that I did not make my morning appointments? I had a lot of questions, but no answers. What about my husband's car, was it ever found?

As the questions flashed through my mind, I wondered if anybody would believe my story?

The doctor from the Rape Crisis Center, along with the young woman, walked into the room. The doctor immediately started his examination. I got the feeling that this was a very familiar procedure for him. He began with the normal line of questions, "Can you get pregnant?"

"No."

"Do you know if the man had an orgasm?" the doctor asked.

I was taken aback by this question. "I really don't know, nor did I really care."

The doctor explained that they would run the normal tests for VD so that if there were traces found, the proper medication could be administered. He collected all of his so-called evidence, being careful for the young woman to document all of his findings. He was very quiet as he worked, except for his point-blank questions. He volunteered an abrupt thank you as he left the room. The young woman stayed behind.

"I contacted your husband. I told him only that you were at Broward General and that you were all right. He is on his way." The room was silent for a second, "I did not tell him about your eyes," she said. "I didn't tell him anything about your condition. I only told him that you were found and that you were here. I didn't want him to get into an accident on the way down."

I thanked her for contacting my family. I told her that I guessed that the hospital staff was so concerned about my physical well-being that they forgot to contact the family.

On her way out she told me that if there was anything else she could do, she would be available. I thanked her again for her help.

A nurse came in to set up an I.V. to prepare me for surgery. I couldn't help wondering how long I had been in the hospital.

"Do you have any idea how long I've been here?"

"Let me see," she said. "The first notation on the chart is 10:45 a.m."

She continued with her work setting up the I.V. She told me that soon I would feel the effects of the I.V. I would start to get woozy as the sedative took hold. I sensed another nurse at the door. There was urgency in her voice as the first nurse left my side to see what she wanted. Once again the first nurse returned.

"Your husband has arrived. Would you like to see him before you go into surgery?"

"Yes, I would."

I heard the sounds of footsteps approaching, slow and heavy. I could sense him peering down at me as I lay there on the stretcher. The nurse stayed in the room.

"Wayne, I'm all right. Really I am. How are the children?"

"The children are fine. I called your mother and father in Ohio when the police told me that you were missing. They're on their way."

I felt my thoughts getting foggy. The sedative was taking hold. I knew that I would soon be out completely. I left Wayne with instructions to contact work and tell them that I would not be in. Tell my parents not to worry. I could hear him starting to sob. Once again I wanted to confirm that I was all right.

"Wayne, everything's going to be just fine, don't worry. I'm getting a little tired now. I'll talk to you later."

I heard his footsteps fade into the distance, and so did the voices. I felt myself getting calm and very tired. Quietly and slowly I drifted off into deep, sedated sleep.

CHAPTER THREE

Independent Study

I spent a week in the hospital recovering from my ordeal. From the first moments of regaining consciousness, I was dogged by the mixed signals which were to be a constant theme in my life for the next years and which—I am sure—inhibit the recovery of almost everyone who has had a traumatic and disabling injury, of everyone who has a handicap. Everyone tried to stamp me with their expectations, their models of what should and should not be, their mental images, their reactions to my injuries and experiences. It was generally well-intentioned, but the only part that is useful to the "victim" is honest praise. Everything else had to be ignored if I were ever to accomplish anything. The mixed signals in my case could be summed up as praising my past and damning my future. I had been a heroine, now I was a victim with nothing before me. It would seem to me to be self-evident that if a person's past is praiseworthy, his or her future is likely to be no less praiseworthy. But others saw with different eyes.

For the first two and half days after I went to surgery, nothing was a problem because I was in intensive care slipping in and out of consciousness. Once when I awoke, I found my parents by my bedside. They had come from Ohio immediately when they heard that I was missing. I can remember my father holding my hand and crying—the first time I had ever heard him cry. It is hard to imagine anything but serious injury to his wife or children which would make him cry. I could say little more than, "I'm fine. Everything is going to be all right." My father and mother both had time to tell me that everything would be fine before consciousness seeped away.

When I awoke, almost immediately those mixed signals began. I could hear but not see movement around me. I reached up to touch the bandages on my eyes.

"Oh, look who's awake." The woman's voice was unfamiliar.

"Where am I?" I asked.

"You are now in your own private room, Sharon. This is where you will be spending the next few days." It felt odd talking to the voices and not seeing the faces.

"So, how is our wonder patient today? You really left quite an impression on the emergency staff. It didn't take long at all for the word to reach all the way around the hospital; they're still talking about you."

I turned my head toward the direction of the nurse's voice and managed a smile, "I don't quite understand, what did I do?"

"You astounded everybody with your courage. They never saw anything quite like it. Let's face it, Sharon, they are not used to somebody coming into a hospital in your condition and still having the presence of mind to talk to the police, the doctors, and everybody. It was you and your reaction. It just isn't something that we see everyday around here."

The other nurse's voice joined the conversation. "Sharon, all you have to do now is relax. We'll be bringing lunch shortly. One more thing before we leave you alone. When you speak with your family, tell them that they will have to ask for your room by number. This is for your own protection. If they ask for your name, the desk downstairs has no information on you, and they'll never get through. Also you have been given an alias name, your hospital records and your armband have been changed to the name of Sherry Halliday. This we understand is being done for security reasons, for your own protection, you know."

I kept quiet for a while listening to their footsteps head towards the door, "Wait a second, what day is today? Were my parents here? Are they in town?"

"Sharon, today is Monday. It's Monday afternoon. You were in intensive care for the past two and a half days, and yes, your mother and father were in to see you late Friday evening. You'll find out more later on. Just for now, relax."

I heard the footsteps leave the room. Everything was still a little foggy. Slowly, I began to make sense of everything. Once again I reached for the bandages on my eyes, I checked them out carefully. There was a hard plastic shell covered over with adhesive tape holding them in place. I touched my hair—still a matted, filthy mess. I wondered if they were going to wash it while I was in the hospital. My parents—I wondered what they were doing in town. The past two and a half days bore only a vague semblance to reality. I remember the buzzer, the footsteps, my father's hand touching mine, my father crying, my mother leaving the room and coming back, both of them telling me that everything was going to be all right. But that was the only recollection I had. Now here I was safe in my hospital bed, no longer fighting for my life, no longer struggling to get free or planning my next move. I was now safe in a hospital bed knowing, without any doubt whatsoever, that I was going to live.

A small bandage covered the stab wound on my chest, another the slash on my neck. Once again I felt over my eyes checking the bandages very carefully. Yes, they were in place. My eyes were closed under the bandages. When the bandages came off and I opened my eyes, what would I see? I remember the doctor vaguely talking about the left eye and no hope, but the right eye was questionable. Why did I have that deep, sinking feeling that what I saw now with my eyes bandaged closed was the same thing I would see for the rest of my life? Why had I already come to that reality? For some reason it felt so final. I knew that I would never see my children again. I knew that I would never drive my car again. I knew, without any doubt, that I would be blind for the rest of my life.

I reached for the lever to raise the head of my bed to a more comfortable position. I adjusted my pillow and the covers and once again settled back to "relax." *"My God, what happened? Life seemed so perfect. I have a new house, good career, three loving children, a husband. What more could I ask for? Who was this man? Where did he find me? Why did he want to do this? Did he mistake me for somebody else? Would the detectives ever find him? Would he victimize somebody else before they did?"* There was nobody around to ask these questions. I knew the answers would have to wait.

I was lying there lost in thoughts about myself, *"But what about my children? How is this going to affect them? And what about Wayne? Did they even know what happened. Did they know that I would never see them again?"*

I reached over for the table next to me and located the phone without any difficulty. I dialed nine for an outside line and continued with my home telephone number. The phone only rang once.

"Hello," my mother was right on top of things, the first one to answer the telephone. I wondered how she beat the children to the phone.

"Hi, Mom, it's me."

"I didn't expect you to call. Are you in your own room now? How are you feeling?"

I could feel the tension in my mother's voice. She was surprised, worried, angered, and she didn't hide her emotions very well. "I'm feeling pretty good, Mom, so don't worry about that. Were you and Dad in here the other night?"

"Yes, we stopped in Friday evening, but that's when you just came out of surgery. You didn't look very good. Do you know when you'll be getting out of there?"

"No, I really don't. How are the children?"

"The children are just fine, don't you worry about them. Just worry about taking care of yourself and getting out of there. Wayne is taking care of all of the paperwork, social security, crime compensation and police reports. There's a lot of paperwork to do. I called Aunt Evelyn to see if she could find a good doctor in the area here. I figured if anybody would know she would. She's having Maryann look into it. I am going to be taking you out of there and getting you to an eye specialist. The doctor said something that maybe your right eye could be saved. We are going to look into this, Sharon. Everything is going to be all right."

I could sense the concern, the take-charge attitude of my mother. This was her way of doing things. I wouldn't expect anything less. I understood her frustration in feeling totally helpless, watching her child lying in the hospital bed suffering in such a fashion, with the possibility of losing her eyesight forever. I also knew that the first person she would call would be my aunt in Ohio since her daughter was a medical student at Ohio State. She was always the first person in the family to be contacted as soon as a medical emergency arose. I knew that the children were well taken care of. My mother is very strong on the outside, but a super-soft, sensitive person on the inside. She has a way of covering up that sensitivity with an armor-plated exterior.

"Sharon, I know you have a lot of questions. The children are here, and they want to talk to you."

"How much do they know, Mom?"

"They only know that you were shot but that you are all right. They don't know anything about the loss of your eyesight yet. Somebody in school told Shawn or Marc, one of them, that you were also stabbed. I just keep reinforcing the fact that you are okay, and that you will be coming home. Their school has been notified and know what's going on, so they are watching them as well."

The next voice on the phone was that of my older son, Shawn. He was only nine years old, but now he was going to be getting a dose of reality—of life as it really is—not all sweet and wonderful, but a lesson in life that certain things are beyond our control and we have to face up to them.

"Hi, Mom, how are you feeling? Are you going to be coming home soon?"

"Hi, Shawn. I'm just fine. I'm not quite sure when I'll be coming home yet. The doctor hasn't let me know yet. How are you guys doing over there? Are you behaving for "Grandma?""

"We're okay, Mom. Grandma's doing just fine. It's nice to see her again. I know before you even ask, Mom, school's okay, too. Kristin's been acting up a little bit, but that's not unusual."

Shawn seemed so intelligent, so much older than his nine years. He was always the big brother taking charge, taking care of his little brother and sister. The thought kept recurring: *"I'll never see him again."*

"Hi, Mom, how are you? Mom, I heard you were stabbed, is that true?"

"Hi, Marc. I'm just fine, don't worry. Yes, I was stabbed, but it was really nothing serious. Are you guys behaving for Grandma?" I knew that one would feel slighted if I didn't ask this question of each. I also knew that I would never get an honest answer, because each one of them individually behaved, naturally. It was always the others who were acting up.

Marc continued on with day-to-day problems with school, homework, his sister, his brother, and all the things that were very important to him. I just lay there quietly in my hospital bed listening to my little boy rattle on and on. The thought again, *"Never see him again."*

"Ma, Kristin's pulling on the telephone cord. I'm going to have to go now, but I'll talk to you later. Is it okay if we call you?"

"Yes, Marc, you can call me. I'll give Grandma the telephone number and my room number. I'll talk to you later. Be good."

"Hi, Mommy, are you feeling okay?" The sound of my little Kristin, my little three year old, her voice was soft, slower speaking, the little angel—only I knew better. She was talking so softly, so sweetly, and only a couple of minutes before I heard her yelling in the background at her brothers who were aggravating her. Just a very normal little three year old.

"How are you, Kris? Are you behaving for Grandma?"

"Yes, Mommy, I'm being a very good girl, but Shawn and Marc keep bothering me. It is nice to see Grandma again. I'm glad she came down to stay with us. When are you coming home?"

"I miss you too, Kris. The doctor didn't tell me when I am going to be able to come home, but as soon as he does, I'll give a call and let you know. I don't think it will be too much longer."

"Well, mommy, grandma's standing here and she wants to talk to you again. I'm going to go play now. I miss you, mom. I'm going to throw you a kiss and a hug."

I heard the smack of her tiny little lips throwing me a kiss, and I heard her grunt in the telephone like she was squeezing it or giving it a hug. Again a thought rang out loud and clear, *"Never see her, never see my little three year old go through all the stages of adolescence to adulthood. Never see her blond hair, her blue eyes, or her smiling face. What would I tell her if she asked me, 'How do I look, Mom?' "*

My mother's voice interrupted my thoughts. "Well, Sharon, you'd better get some rest now. You've been talking long enough. I'll give you a call later."

"Mom, by the way, they changed my name in the hospital. My name is now Sherry Halliday, but that's only for the record keeping. When you call here, ask for the room number, otherwise it won't go through. It's okay to let the children call, mom. Really it is."

My mother told me she would be coming down for visiting hours. I asked her to please bring my shampoo, conditioner and blow dryer. I couldn't stand my hair anymore the way it was, still matted, dirty. You would think the hospital would have washed it by now. She told me she would also bring a change of clothes, that everything was going to be okay.

I hung up the telephone and pushed it back on the table. I noticed some noise out in the hallway, a nurse was bringing a tray in. "It's time for lunch," she said as she walked into the room. She pulled over the sliding table and put the tray down.

"Well, Sharon, here's your first meal. Let me help you. When they start teaching you how to be blind, they're going to teach you how to eat according to the face of the clock. Let me explain." The nurse continued telling me where everything was. The vegetables were at three o'clock, the meat was at seven o'clock. The potatoes were at twelve o'clock. There was bread off to my left, utensils to my right, a cup of tea at the top. She arranged everything for me accordingly. She removed any obstacles in my way, prepared my tea, including the sugar and cream, then left me with the instructions that when I was finished, I could just ring the buzzer for her. She would then return to remove the tray.

I heard her footsteps leave the room. I just sat there quietly for a moment, thinking. *"Teach me how to be blind?"* I reached for my silverware off to the left, placed the napkin in my lap. Everything was already done for me; the meat was cut, my tea was prepared. What would happen when I had to do this myself? At least I had no difficulty finding my mouth, eating would be absolutely no problem. I finished, then rang the buzzer for the nurse to return. She picked up the tray and left.

Once again I settled back in bed. Once again I was alone, no one to talk to, nothing to read, nothing to listen to, plenty of time to return to the wondering that I had been doing all along.

Some say that thinking can be detrimental to one's mental health, especially when you have idle time on your hands. I had no one around to offer suggestions as to how I was supposed to act or react to what had happened, no one to tell me how he would handle my situation. I valued my time alone, to lie there and think things through. I felt this was going to be very important for me. I could believe those words, "Everything will be just fine," I knew it was just a matter of time. The real question was: How much time?

Every now and then a nurse would pop in to see how I was doing. She would check my pulse, take my temperature and blood pressure. The evening meal was brought and followed the same routine as lunch. Everything was done for me.

As I lay there I could analyze the steps in the hall, the noises in the hospital. I knew the voice of every nurse who attended me. There was more confusion in the hallway than usual and then I heard my mother's voice at the door.

"Sharon, it's Mom, how are you feeling?"

I assumed that it must have been visiting hours. I greeted my Mother, she told me that she had brought all of my requests, shampoo, conditioner, blow dryer, change of clothes. Wayne's voice quickly followed with a gentle kiss on the cheek. They told me that everything was in order at home. There were forms to be filled out, formalities to be taken care of, and they were doing just that. Wayne had brought along some of the paperwork that required my signature.

Then my mother got very serious. She told me that she had spoken to the doctor and had offered one of her eyes if it was necessary to restore the sight in my right eye. She knew that there was a glimmer of hope. She was determined that I was going to see again.

My mother had also spoken to the detectives. I knew she wanted to know everything that was going on. She told me that the man had been apprehended. She did not know all the details, but I knew that she would find them out as quickly as she could. She had even asked the detectives if she could go down to the city jail to talk to the man who attacked her daughter. The police would not allow it.

I was relieved that the man was off the streets, but I still had many questions. They would have to wait until I talked to the detectives.

Wayne told me that he picked up the car from the police pound, and its condition was not very good. It was covered with black dust inside where the police dusted for fingerprints. The upholstery and the steering wheel were covered with my blood. The police cut a hole in the roof on the passenger side to remove a bullet that had lodged in the roof rail above the passenger's window. The car would need some repair work. I gave Wayne the name of a bodyshop man I knew from work.

I asked him about my job. He said that he had contacted them, and that they would have all of my things removed from my desk immediately and that my mother and he would go down to pick them up.

Here was another signal. What good is a blind insurance adjuster? I was through, fired, and my things were to be removed immediately. "We are sorry"? Never spoken. "We will always have a place for you if you want to work"? Never mentioned. "We have a plan that covers your need"? Not they, they were only an insurance company, after all. So all those years of work, of studying for exams, of qualifying for a license had ended in this. My desk would be cleared immediately—no obligations and no need for me to take up space any longer. So far as my employer was concerned, I was rendered useless forever.

Wayne and my mother reassured me that the household was running smoothly, that the children were taken care of, and that all the formalities were in hand. Wayne said that he received a telephone call from the Division of Blind Services in Palm Beach County, and that as soon as I was back at home, they would visit me to start me on my road to rehabilitation. This was another bad signal, although I did not recognize it at the time.

"Well, Sharon, is there anything else you need?" my mother asked.

"I really don't think so, mom, you can't bring me any magazines to read." My mother did not chuckle at my sense of humor. After all, this was not a laughing matter. I asked Wayne if there was a way to get a television in my room. I wanted to keep up on the local news broadcasts and even the soap operas. Quickly, Wayne went out and checked with the nurse. I would have one in my room first thing in the morning.

The loudspeaker told us, "Visiting hours are now over."

"Well, Sharon, we'll see you tomorrow." My mother reached over, touched me on the hand, gave me a kiss on the cheek and a hug. I heard my mother's footsteps head for the door. Wayne reached over, touched my hand, gave me a kiss on the cheek, told me that he would see me tomorrow also. I heard his footsteps, the longer, more solid stride, head towards the door. Once again I was left alone.

It was an odd feeling not knowing whether it was dark outside or light, whether the lights inside were on or off. With my eyes shut underneath heavy bandages, there was no way to tell whether even a shadow would get through.

My hands reached up toward my head. It was absolutely amazing, I thought. How freakish this whole thing was. Instantly I flashed back to my last sight. The road in front of me, the flash of light out of the side vision on my left, and then nothing. I knew I was traveling between 45 and 50 miles an hour. I couldn't help wondering what the odds were of the whole thing happening exactly as it did that night, again. That bullet passed through so cleanly, through both eyes. I did not even need stitches where the bullet went in and came out. There was no other physical damage to any other facial feature. No brain damage. And best of all, I was still alive. Why? Could there possibly be some unknown reason for this whole thing happening? How could there possibly be any sense in this totally senseless act?

My thoughts turned to the past. Growing up in a suburb outside of Cleveland. The word "blind" kept ringing loud and clear. When I was younger, my mother and I would take trips to downtown Cleveland during Christmas time. I saw the same blind man, year after year, on the corner with his tin cup in hand, his dog at his feet and his cane stretched out in front of him. Would that be me? I always felt so sorry for him. Never seeing the beautiful sunrises, the multi-colors in a rainbow, the smile on children's faces. As I passed by all the multi-colored lights in the shop windows, watched all the little characters running to and fro in the Christmas displays, I couldn't help wondering what it would be like never to see that. I would walk up, touch the plain glass—me—knowing what was behind there, but that poor man—never being able to see was frightening. I remember thinking that the worst thing that could ever happen to me would be to lose my sight. And now, here I was. It was no longer a possibility. It was reality.

It seemed cold comfort to go to sleep on such a thought, but I know now that I was doing the best thing I could for myself. I was sending the signals, and I was sending myself the most productive signal I possibly could: Live with reality. Perhaps I had been lucky in my choice of career. As an insurance adjuster, I had to assess the damage and determine what it would take to get everything running again. Now I had to do it with my own life.

The next morning, I had another signal from a doctor with a sense of purpose but no vision. He arrived on his morning rounds when I was halfway through breakfast. He took off the bandages and again I could feel the warmth of his light as he peered inside my damaged eyes.

"Sharon, we have to talk about this now."

Once again, I had the deep, sinking feeling that I knew exactly what was coming.

"I don't want you to hold out any false hopes. There is no chance of restoring your sight." There was a lull in the conversation, as though he was waiting for some sort of a reaction.

"Yes, doctor, I sort of felt that already."

"No, Sharon, you don't understand. You will never see again."

And, once again I told the doctor that I knew exactly what he was saying.

He continued, "I want you to start on your rehabilitation right away, I don't want you to waste any time. People like you can always find your own plane of existence. I want you to face up to the reality right away, Sharon. You will never see again."

I tried to tell the doctor again that I understood him. And, that in my own way, I had already started my own rehabilitation. In his tone I could sense the skepticism. Maybe I was handling this whole thing too well for his liking. It was my way of dealing with what had happened.

Quickly and curtly, the doctor told me about the conversation he had with my mother. She wanted another opinion. He said that would be fine with him. He was arranging for my release on Friday, barring any unforeseen circumstances. The neurosurgeon would be in for a visit to see how I was doing. At that time he would decide finally about my release on Friday. His tone was cold. His bedside manner left a lot to be desired. I was offended by his words and tone. He said he would see me tomorrow and left.

I continued with my morning breakfast. I thought to myself for a while and muttered quietly to myself, "Isn't he sweet!"

"Did you say something, Sharon?" The nurse was still in the room.

I asked her about this doctor who seemed so cold.

"He's had a pretty rough week, he's been working an awful lot with gunshot cases. Your case affected him. He couldn't restore your sight even though he wanted to. Sharon, he really wanted you to see again. It was totally out of his control. He really is a good doctor, and a very nice man as well."

I sat there listening to the words of the nurse. I admitted to her that I was probably guilty of rash judgment. She took my tray and left the room. I guess I could understand his frustrations. It was his way of dealing with the crisis. I put myself in his position. It must not be easy being a doctor faced with the reality of your own human limitations. There was only so much that could be done, and I know that he did his best. In his own way, he wanted me to get on with life. And he was telling me that the only way that he knew how. As cold as it may have seemed, that was his way.

The rest of the morning was filled with other visitors, including the detectives, Russo and Haas. They took my statement as promised. They also informed me that my attacker had been apprehended. They told me that they found a personal telephone book when they collected the evidence in the apartment where Charlie had taken them. They started calling all of the telephone numbers and finally reached one where my attacker was staying. The voice on the other end of the phone told them that he was asleep. The police said not to wake him, that they would call later. They then traced the telephone number, and went to the location. They told me how they caught him as he was fleeing with the plastic trash bag that I had told them about. They found that car, the dark-colored, early-model Maverick with one working headlight. My blood was all over the back seat.

The positive identification of the car dispelled any fears that I had that two men might be involved. The police told me that the bullet was fired from the car which was following mine and started to overtake me on the left. It was fired by the man who was driving that vehicle. And the same man who was driving that vehicle kidnapped me and took me to his apartment.

I thanked the police for their efforts and told them how relieved I was that the man was off the streets. They told me that they would be in contact in preparation for the trial. There were still legal formalities to take care of. They would need more blood samples, hair samples, and even fingerprints. All that would be taken care of at a later date.

After they left, I turned on the television. When I grew tired of listening to it, I returned to my quiet moments, to my own rehabilitation: The self-analysis; the self-questioning; confronting head-on any feelings or emotions that were disturbing; never denying what had happened; analyzing every step of that night; reminding myself over again that it was just a freak attack. I did nothing wrong. The only way it could have been prevented was by not being there in the first place. I started to face those deep, dark questions that every person asks when they are faced with a tragedy. *"Why did this have to happen to me? What if I had not been driving alone that night?"* And going back even further, *"What if I had never moved from Ohio to Florida?"* I never thought that I would ever be a victim of crime. It always happened to someone else. I read the headlines in the newspaper, listened to the six and eleven o'clock news tell of the heinous crimes that had been committed. But it always seemed so far removed. I asked myself why I felt that it could never happen to me? I was just like everyone else, exposed to the same things, taking all the same risks on a daily basis. I went back to that same question: *"Why me? Why not? It was nothing personal. It did not matter who I was or what part of town I lived in or how much money I had. There was no reason in singling me out."* I had to realize that it was something that just happened, it was not under my control. I then examined the question, *"What if? If I had not moved from Ohio to Florida, I would have probably been miserable. It was something I really wanted to do. And I decided to take that risk. There is nothing wrong with moving from one state to another. People do it all the time. If I hadn't been driving alone that night, this whole thing wouldn't have happened. How silly to even think that way. If it hadn't been that night, it could have possibly been another night. I was always on the road, day and evening. There was nothing unusual about that night. I couldn't help being a little amused by that question, 'What if?' "* We have such 20/20 hindsight, after something happens. I could continue to ask, "What if?" forever. What good would it really do? The question I should be asking myself is, "What am I going to do from now on?"

My thoughts were invariably interrupted by the nurses' daily routines. A nurse came in and granted my request to wash my hair. It felt so good to get that dried blood finally rinsed out.

When the doctor made his morning rounds the next day, he said that he hadn't even realized that I had blond hair. He told me I looked different. We had a very pleasant conversation. I semi-apologized for being as short with him as I was. And he semi-apologized for being as curt with me as he was. He stressed that he just didn't want me to hold onto any false hopes. And I explained to him that I really had come to terms with the blindness, but that there was really nothing I could do until I was released from the hospital.

He told me of his frustration in trying to save my eyesight. It was exactly as the nurse explained. I was glad that I spoke with him. I couldn't help thinking that this one crime victimized not only me but many others, each in different ways.

This day was filled with little time for thinking. After the CAT scan was done, the neurosurgeon made his rounds and visited and explained the need for the scan. The path of the bullet was very close to the brain. They wanted to be positive there was no neurological damage. We briefly discussed the things that could have happened. There could have been brain damage, a permanent spinal injury, even death. So many things could have happened, but didn't. Just before the doctor left, he said there was no problem with releasing me on Friday, and that there would be no need for a follow-up visit with him. He wished me well and left.

Only during my last night in the hospital did I begin to think about other people's attitudes and feelings about what had happened to me, particularly about the sexual violation, which had very little meaning to me. How would people on the outside look at me? Would they feel in some way that I was responsible? I couldn't help reviewing the events of that night. *"In that man's apartment, could I have done something to prevent the rape? Should I feel guilt, for letting him? So many times in the past I had heard that no decent woman would ever let a man violate her in such a fashion. What choice did I have? When I became very aggressive with him, as when he started to suffocate me with a pillow, he became very aggressive with me. And then again, when I backed off a little, as when I went limp and asked him what he was doing, he became more passive. If I would have kept up that hard aggressive line of attack against him, would I have brought on my own death? I had lived. I had survived the attack; I was alive, so I did everything right. There was no point in feeling guilty for living."* I had to face facts, people were going to express their opinions whether I liked it or not. But I was the one who counted, and I felt comfortable with my actions.

As for being blind, I knew that I could tell my mother and Wayne and the children that I was just fine, that we were going to make it, that everything was going to be all right. But telling them meant little. Unless I followed it up with action, they would never believe me. I knew in my heart that it would not be easy. I really had my work cut out for me. I would listen to what the rehabilitation services offered, listen to their suggestions, but, ultimately, I had to do what was right for me. I didn't know how, or even how long it was going to take. Eventually, I would adjust to the loss of sight, and I would do everything it was possible for a human to do without sight.

As for the man who attacked me, he took ten hours of my life and my eyesight. I was determined not to give him any more of my time. I knew that if I kept anger locked up inside of me and if that anger kept me from being a useful person, I would be giving him more time than he deserved. I wanted to be selfish with that time. It was going to be used for me and my children and my family. I didn't want to waste that time on him. He had taken too much already.

CHAPTER FOUR

Creative Problem Solving

When I left the hospital, I knew about four problems facing me: My children, my blindness, my employment, and my attacker. I did not know that several other severe problems lurked in the darkness: My husband, other people, and the social welfare agencies. Of all these problems, only two were under my immediate control: My children and my adaptation to blindness. Those were the most urgent problems, and I dealt with them the most successfully.

Throughout my ordeal, my constant concern was to get home to my children. Now, as I was driven home, they were there to greet me with their hugs and kisses which are as dear to me as life itself. I knew that the first thing I had to do was to talk with them. They had to be reacquainted with their mother in her new state. I sat all three of them on the couch and explained to them very carefully what had happened. I didn't want to leave any questions unanswered in their little minds. I couldn't take the chance that they would be misinformed by a schoolmate. I knew how cruel comments from little children could be. I wanted my children to have all the facts and to have them straight. I knew also that I could not wait for them to hear things from other children.

I told them about the drive home, about being shot and kidnapped. I told them that I was in the man's apartment, but that I had escaped. I was taken to the hospital and was now safe at home with them. I gave them only the information that I felt they were capable of handling at their young ages. The main focus was on my loss of sight. Things would have to change within the household. I explained to little Kristin how toys would have to be picked up, cupboard doors would have to be closed, and the boys would have to be responsible for shutting off lights. I explained to them that even when the bandages came off, I would still be blind.

" Mom, you mean the doctors say that you'll never see again?"

"Yes, Marc, the doctors say I will never see again."

"Boy, what a birthday present." Marc's eighth birthday was only a couple of weeks away.

"Marc, look at it this way, I lost my sight, but I came very close to not being here at all. I came very close to not even sharing your birthday with you this year. Isn't it more important that I am here with you?"

Quietly, somberly, Marc replied, "I guess you're right, mom." He reached over and gave me a hug, "I really am glad you're here, mom, even if you can't see. You're right, it's more important for you to be alive and still here with us."

We all discussed how things were going to change. Because I could no longer drive my car, I would not be driving on field trips. And I would no longer be working. I told them that I was now going to need their help, that they were going to have to be my eyes. And that we would all do it together. I could not expect them to understand fully everything all at once. Right now, the focus was that I was at home with them. I knew there would be frustrating times when they would forget little things; I couldn't expect them to adapt immediately. There was no way that I could anticipate problems. I knew that we would have to handle them as they arose.

Ever since that day, my children and I have worked together very productively. So adaptable and creative are children that we have contrived to turn my blindness into an asset for them. As they have functioned as my eyes, they have become more articulate, more observant, more creative, more confident, more self-reliant, and more responsible. Shawn and Marc are in the gifted program (Kristin gets tested next year), and all three do well in school. I may not be able to judge their penmanship, but I have been able to encourage them to excel. And they remain the center of my life, the touchstone by which I value all that happens and any opportunities that might arise. Having nearly been lost to them, I have never been willing to put myself in a position in which I might be lost to them for long periods of time for any benefit—economic or otherwise. I have endeavored to make our home the center of values and accurate information for their lives. Too frequently in the first months after my injury, they came home with misinformation from other children. I would then set about improving their education and incidentally letting them know that they could always get the correct information at home.

My children are a major reason why I was not devastated by my blindness. Certainly there is deprivation, loss, inconvenience, and much more that comes with blindness. But it was no longer the most horrible thing that could possibly happen to me—as it had been in my childish imagination when I watched the little blind girl with the glazed look play her guitar on television. "My God, how horrible!" had become, "It could have been worse."

In dealing with my blindness, I broke down the problems into parts and solved them one by one. I completely deferred the question of earning a living until after the trial. I knew that I would need to concentrate all my attention on my testimony and anything else I could do to put this man away. He must never menace me again. Because my attempts to earn a living would suffer at that time, it seemed better to put aside my livelihood.

My first problem with blindness was mobility in the house. We had bought the house eight months earlier, and I knew the floor plan and the furnishings. I walked around the walls trailing my hands until I was confident in my ability to navigate. Because I had lost my sight, I had to move slower and concentrate more. I cannot walk aimlessly. I must pay attention to every step, every movement. The sheer mental energy that movement requires leaves me tired every evening. I need a good night's sleep to maintain my concentration and my mobility.

Movement outside the house is accomplished by holding onto the arm of the person leading me. There have been some interesting moments, such as when my children walked under branches that passed over their heads and smacked into mine. However, they soon learned about low branches, steps, curbs, mud puddles, cracks in the sidewalk, and other hazards—and I did not lose any teeth or break any toes in the process. We kept these little learning experiences a joke so they did not have guilty consciences about marching mommy into a tree. Almost any emotion is more productive than guilt.

I had heard tales that blind people have special senses, that they are able to feel things that sighted people cannot. I remember well the first time that my mother and I went for a walk around the block. We were on the sidewalk a few feet from the curb. At one point I asked my mother if we had just passed a car parked at the curb. "How did you know?" My mother was clearly surprised. I told her that it sounded different, that I could hear the emptiness, but when we came to the car, it just sounded like there was something there, and then once we passed it, it was just open again. It was not that I added a sense, it was only that I concentrated my attention and could hear differences in sound that a sighted person would not need to heed.

If I could move, I figured I could tend to my own personal care. There is no big trick to brushing your teeth without vision—as long as you are careful to squeeze the toothpaste tube and not the rubbing ointment or some other vile tasting substance. I could shower, wash, dry myself, and dress with only minor alterations in my routine. Combing my hair was somewhat harder, and I had to moderate my use of make-up. I could apply some but not a lot. I found the bed as easy to make as ever. I could do some straightening and cleaning in the rest of the house, but I am not very good at waxing or polishing until I can see myself. With a little effort, I can iron and do basic mending with a sewing needle. My ability to thread a needle has not improved, and the sewing machine is a tool I regard with the same feeling as I have for a jack hammer—let somebody else do the heavy work. When Kristin needs a patch on her Brownie uniform, she brings me everything I need, positions the patch, and lets me go to work. The results are probably no worse than those of many other mothers.

The first morning I was home from the hospital, I got a series of lessons in blindness—all before I finished tea. When I had finished dressing and putting on my make-up, I went into the kitchen and called for my mother. She was not there, so I figured there was no time like the present to start myself on my own "road to rehabilitation," as the doctor had put it. I took the teapot and filled it with water, got out my own cup, put the teabag in, turned on the stove and waited for the water to boil. I took two pieces of bread from the wrapper and placed them in the toaster. I opened the refrigerator door and felt for the butter. It was not in its usual place. I began feeling along the counters. I found it by sticking my fingers in it. I knew that the children would not mind and would probably assume that I had put the fingerprint in the butter. I listened to the water in the pot coming to a simmer and then a full boil. I turned the knob all the way around until it clicked into the off position. I heard the toast pop up, took it out of the toaster and put it onto a plate. I reached for a knife to spread the softened butter over the toast. This is going to be easy, I thought. I reached for the teapot being careful not to burn myself on the side. I had no trouble locating the handle. Carefully and slowly I poured the boiling water into my teacup. I remembered watching other blind people put their fingers inside the cup to measure the distance to the top. I did the same. I quickly found out that you could get burnt fingertips that way.

I let the teabag steep awhile, put my usual half-teaspoonful of sugar and a little bit of milk in my cup and stirred it slowly. My very first breakfast, and it was not that difficult.

I heard the door slam and quickly turned. My mother heard the crash come from the kitchen. "Are you all right? What are you doing in there?"

My hand had hit the edge of the spoon that I left in my cup. I hit it hard enough so the spoon, the teacup and its contents all landed on the floor. *"I was doing so well."*

My mother came running into the kitchen. "What do you think you're doing? You know I would fix breakfast for you. You should have waited until I came back in. Go sit down. I'll clean this up. Let me take care of you. Go sit down!"

I felt like a child being reprimanded. Very carefully and cautiously, even more so than before, I trailed along the counters over to the kitchen table and sat down. My first attempt at the kitchen, and it was shattered. I spoke up. "But mom, it's only a broken cup. It can be cleaned up. I have plenty of them."

"But you could have gotten hurt, you could have burned yourself with the boiling water. You could have cut yourself on the glass," my mother answered back.

I knew that she was right. Those things could have happened, but how else was I going to learn if I didn't do it for myself? I had to find my own ways even if it bothered those who were watching me. I asked myself how to say no to my mother without hurting her feelings when I don't want help?

My mother finished fixing me another cup of tea. She made herself one and sat down at the kitchen table. Very quietly I told my mother there were certain things that I was going to have to do for myself. I asked her what would happen when she left and I was alone.

Her answer was quick. I should move back to Ohio so she could be there all the time to help me. While the idea had some merit, we had moved to Florida for the children's health—they had severe allergies which were not a problem in Florida but were crippling in Ohio. No advantage from a move is worth risking your children's health. We would not move back.

Now I was getting a dose of a new problem: Other people. While I love my mother and she loves me, the essence of our transaction could have discouraged most disabled people from trying to do everything they can possibly do. I was concerned that it not happen to me, whether my mother or anyone else was offering to do for me things that I knew I would eventually have to do for myself.

I had anticipated getting help in dealing with my blindness from the Division of Blind Services. They were a terrible disappointment because they did not care about me. They had their own agenda and their own way of justifying themselves to their funding sources. They were determined to offer their program whether it met my needs or not. When they arrived for their first visit nearly a month after I had been blinded, it soon became obvious that their representatives were not thinking very clearly. The woman who was to be my instructor was legally blind. The woman who accompanied her was her driver.

My instructor explained the difference between legally blind and totally blind. She was still able to read large print, see vague shapes and differentiate black and white images. I was totally blind. She had me tell a little about myself, first what I did before I was shot, and then a little bit about what had happened, the incident that had taken my sight. She explained that blind people can be rehabilitated and worked into the mainstream of life once again, with some limitations.

She handed me some cassette tapes. They were on inside mobility, how to reteach myself to walk within my own environment. They would give me some tips and guidelines. I was already doing very well in my house. Anything I needed to learn about inside mobility I had bumped into or tripped over more than three weeks ago.

My instructor continued. She told me how they would teach me how to brush my teeth, take a shower and wash my hair. *"I have done all of these things. What does she think I've been doing for the past three weeks? If I had not learned these arts, it would not have been very pleasant to be in the same room with me!"* She explained how they would teach me to become a very normal human being once again. They would teach me Braille and since there would be no longer any use for me writing, not to worry about it. Supposedly within four or five months, I would forget how to write anyhow. They would, however, show me the proper way to sign my name as a blind person. There would be various gadgets and paraphernalia for my use. I would now be eligible from the telephone company for free unlimited directory assistance. She would help me fill out the application to obtain a handicap sticker for the vehicle that would be driving me. I would also be registered to attend a fourteen-week session given by the Rehabilitative Services in Daytona Beach.

She took my measurements for a white cane with a red tip—one that would designate that I was blind. She told me that this cane would be my protection and that every driver should know that it is a federal offense to hit a person using this white cane. I had just been given a good lesson on how much fear of the law protected me. I knew that I would rely on the cane to protect me when crossing a street when I was ready to have, "But She Was In The Right," engraved on my tombstone. She continued that in Daytona Beach, they would teach me how to cross a four-lane highway by myself. That was something I did not do when I had full vision, and I could not imagine why I would want to try it blind. They would teach me independent living skills, how to climb up and down steps. I had already figured that out for myself. There, in Daytona, they would teach me once again how to be an independent human being. She also said she had information about guide dogs. I would go to the city where their training facility was and spend another six weeks learning how to use the dog. There was still so much that I could do, she reassured. They had been very successful in rehabilitating people who had gone blind. She told me clerks in the coffee shop of the courthouse were blind. There were typists who were totally blind. I, too, could still be a useful part of society.

Our first meeting was short; weekly lessons would begin a week later. She promised I could start my lessons with Braille. She would also sign me up for the Talking Book Program. I would be able to receive any books I wanted on tape. She said there was a catalog available and that I could receive any type of travel aids or items specifically designed for the blind. These would include timers for baking, special measuring cups and spoons and various other calibrated measuring devices with tactile rather than visual guides. She reminded me that as soon as an opening was available, I could go to Daytona for the fourteen-week rehabilitative session.

The entire session did not sit well with me. I had been looking forward to help for me, not to hearing a script on helping a handicapped person. None of what the Division of Blind Services had to offer made any sense for me except the application forms for free directory assistance calls, handicapped parking sticker, talking books, and a few of the mechanical aids. The seeing-eye dog we discussed was out: Marc's allergies were too bad. Braille would be a silly thing for me to try to learn: It is a communication system made obsolete by the prevalence of cassette recorders. I could get anything I wanted to hear in recorded form, and I could use my recorder to take notes. A fourteen-week course away from my children was equally useless. The Division of Blind Services would make no provision to look after my children. "That is your problem," they told me, "We only look after the blind person, not the family." I had fought to be reunited with my family. What my attacker failed to achieve, the Division of Blind Services proposed to do by way of helping me.

When at subsequent sessions I told the Division's personnel that I would not learn Braille nor attend their fourteen-week course, they became argumentative and hostile. Never once did they propose that we sit down and construct a program that would make sense for me. They reiterated that I had to learn Braille and that I had to go to Daytona for fourteen weeks, otherwise there was nothing that they could do for me.

There was, however, one thing that they could do for me. They had a machine called an Opticon which could scan a line and give a tactile image of a letter—the machine would pass over the letter "T" and would raise some metal bars to make a letter that the blind person could feel. I knew that this would be much easier for me than learning an entirely new alphabet. However, I encountered nothing but resistance in trying to obtain instruction on this machine unless I would agree to learn Braille first. I pointed out that the two systems had little to do with each other. I encountered more resistance. The only thing that I could figure was that they wanted me to learn Braille so that they could lock me in for the rest of my life to their "services." Finally, after spending more time and energy arguing than the machine was worth, I got some lessons on the Opticon. I mastered it easily and in far less time than is allotted in the Division's lessons. At the point that I mastered the machine, the Division took the machine away from me. Their arguments that I would never be able to master it had been incorrect; to leave the machine in my hands would be enduring proof of their failure of vision. After that I simply gave up dealing with them. They had nothing to offer me. They took my time making me plead for what they should have given me in the first place. They wasted my time teaching me a machine on which they fully expected me to fail and then took the machine away when I succeeded. They are aptly named the Division of Blind Services because they are totally without any vision—they are certainly not the Division of Services for Blind People.

Alas, this Division of Blind Services was not the only social agency to do me a major disservice. There would be others who would attack me with their forms, regulations, rules, and pettiness. In all cases, they sought to reinforce and expand the disability caused by my blindness. None of the social agencies ever made any attempt to help me become a fully functioning, independent human being. They did not help for one of two reasons. Either it was in their best interests to have me dependent upon them for the rest of my life or they had no space or box on their forms that would allow them to take the action that would be really helpful.

Another problem which I did not foresee arose from the attitudes and actions of some people. They did not waste my time and frustrate my efforts on the scale of the Blind Division—it took an entire bureaucracy to be that malevolent—but they individually or in groups conveyed a low estimate of me, for my feelings, and for my ability to be a whole person. When you are recovering from a permanent injury, such low estimates are unwelcome. I had reacted badly in the hospital when the doctor had spoken about "people such as yourself" finding a niche. Now, I began to confront other words that indicated that same low estimate.

My neighbors were the first people I dealt with outside the hospital. Many came over to express the sorrow and grief at what had happened to me and to assure me that they stood by to help in any way that would be useful whether it be rides to the store, helping with the shopping, or looking after the children. They offered love and sympathy freely, and I was delighted that they cared and took the time and trouble to express it. In the years to come, I would be grateful to many of them for their help. I also remember vividly one woman—after expressing her sorrow and sympathy—who turned to my mother as if I were not there at all and asked, "How is Sharon really doing?" as though only those who could see could judge. In departing, this same woman told me, "Oh, my dear, don't worry about things. You will just learn how to cope with them. I'm sure that you will. You seem to be doing just fine."

I was offended that she asked my mother rather than asking me directly, but I guess I was going to have to make concessions for this type of mentality. People were going to stop seeing me because I was blind, and I would have to face it. I decided that I had two choices when confronted by this again: I could take it home with me and let it bother me and dwell upon it indignantly, or I could just overlook it. I decided that I would not be responsible for the insensitivity or ignorance of others.

I cannot abide that word, "cope." I heard it used so many times before. People learn to "cope" with their situation. To me "cope" means to put up with or merely to tolerate the situation. This is something I really didn't want to do. I knew that I would have to find a way to overcome what had happened. The loss of sight was reality. Nothing could possibly change it. I would have to live with it for the rest of my life, and merely to put up with it seemed inadequate. And how could I possibly just cope with the idea of the attack? It was something that I had to put in the past as well. It was just something that happened. It was over and done with. And dwelling on it would really make me disabled. I resolved that I would cope with nothing. I would confront and overcome or else ignore things other people might cope with.

CHAPTER FIVE

Communication Skills

The low estimate of me that I sensed in some people became a problem at home also. I knew we were in trouble within a week of my release from the hospital when my husband told me, "I never knew how much I needed you." I remember my health teacher in high school telling the class that mature love—the kind that sustains through tragedies that can separate two people—is the type of love where one says, "I need you because I love you rather than I love you because I need you." It would have been so much better for us if Wayne had talked about "love" rather than "need." I had the feeling that Wayne was being very accurate in his use of "need" rather than love. How much "needed" work could a blind wife do? The list of needed things I could no longer do was now very long: Grocery shopping, running errands, ferrying the kids around, holding up our share of the car pools, and on and on.

Increasingly, Wayne was retreating into silence, and silence is a totally non-productive way of communicating with a blind person. What was right and what was wrong in our family really became clear when we took our summer vacation in Ohio. The children went ahead with my mother, so Wayne and I flew North just at the Independence Day weekend.

Chuck, a friend from my past job, drove us to the airport. Chuck was always there to help—a true friend. He assisted Wayne with the baggage and also guided me from ticket counter to the gate. The jetway was a problem only occasionally when Wayne would forget to tell me where the floor level would drop at a steep angle, then I would grasp his arm more tightly, and he would apologize for forgetting. On board, he sat me down, made sure that I was comfortable, and then placed our luggage in the overhead bin. I fastened my seatbelt and just waited. I heard Wayne pick up a magazine, and wondered what I was going to do to pass my time. I started to analyze every new sound. I felt the plane shake and begin to move. I heard the flight attendant's voice on the loudspeaker briefing the passengers on safety procedures. I visualized what I had seen done before, the flight attendant standing in the middle of the aisle pointing to the overhead bins where the gold cup would fall with the elastic band that would be used as an oxygen mask, "in the unlikely event of the loss of cabin pressure," holding up the bottom seat cushion with the straps to place your arms through, "in the unlikely event of a water landing." I could visualize her pointing to the front and the rear and the window exits. I could hear the snap of the seat belts followed by the instructions on how to, "insert the flat metal tip into the buckle and pull up on the flat end of the buckle for easy release." She finished her little presentation by thanking everyone for flying the airline. Then the voice on the loudspeaker changed. The co-pilot stated that we were ready for takeoff. I heard sounds I had never heard before. I wondered if they were normal. There was really no way for me to tell. I checked my seatbelt to make sure it was securely fastened, braced myself for takeoff, and closed my eyes, why I don't know. I guess it was just a reflex action.

The captain's voice came over the loudspeaker once again. "We are now over Lake Okeechobee." I turned my head in the direction of the window and placed my hand up against the glass. Sightseeing was definitely going to be out. I recalled my first flight—in November of 1978. I was flying to Fort Lauderdale to check out the area to find a place for the family to live. I flew in at night. I remember being amazed by the sights below. There would be total black darkness everywhere and then off in the distance was a scattering of light all condensed into one area. It looked like billions of stars twinkling below rather than above and the closer we got the more defined each became. From now on all I would be left with was that total darkness.

The flight attendants brought around our beverage and then lunch. Wayne helped me unwrap my silverware and poured the salad dressing on my salad so I would not miss. We talked about what we were going to do when we arrived in Ohio. The flight attendants then returned to take our trays. There was silence once again between us; I could hear the turning of pages and I assumed that Wayne had resumed reading his magazine.

About an hour and a half was left to the trip. Once again I returned to my thoughts, analyzing every movement of the plane, and picking up every conversation of the people around me. What else was there for me to do? I blocked out the voices and the movement, and I lost myself in thoughts of Ohio and the way that things were before. I was going back home to the house where I was raised. I couldn't help wondering what it would be like. I would be sleeping in my old room. I knew every inch of that house. I remember practicing my baton in my mother's living room and being responsible for some of the nicks on the furniture. Baton twirling was a very important part of my life from the time I was twelve years old.

"Look at the Judge, and smile. Don't look at your baton. You should be able to do this with your eyes closed," my teacher would say. I remember freezing on the football field during those chilly fall nights at the high school football game. The highlight of the high school years was performing in front of the sellout crowd at Cleveland stadium at the Browns playoff game, marching down the field with the band, and performing solo during the pregame festivities in my senior year. My mind wandered over all those solo performances, the competition, and the hundreds of trophies. Until the day I moved to Florida, I still taught and judged. My students were so excited when I finally had Kristin, my own little daughter to follow in her mother's footsteps. I remember buying her first baton at our national championships in Philadelphia. She really seemed to like all the glitter of the brightly colored costumes and stood by my side, intensely watching every move of the little girls when they performed. She even tried to mimic their movements with her own little baton. I knew that some day . . . but those images of the past and some day faded into the bleak reality of today.

"We are starting our descent into the Cleveland area and we will make our final approach in about fifteen minutes. Please be sure that your seatbelts are securely fastened and observe the no smoking signs when they are illuminated by the Captain." I searched for a tissue in my purse to dry my eyes. I then touched at my makeup and brushed my hair. I heard Wayne return the magazine to the seat pocket in front of him. He placed his hand on mine. "Are you all right?" He could tell if something was wrong; he could not pry any further.

"Yes, I'm all right." I quickly changed the subject, "How does the weather look out there?"

"It looks a little cloudy, could you expect Cleveland to be anything else?" Neither Wayne nor I had any regrets on the move to Florida. We both enjoyed the sunshine and really didn't miss the gloominess or winters of the Cleveland area. Still it was nice to go home for a visit.

Wayne waited for the plane to empty before he stood up to get our overhead luggage. I stood up and followed close behind touching the back of his jacket until there was enough room for me to move alongside to reach his arm. My brother, Rick, was waiting for us at the end of the jetway. He greeted me with a hug and a kiss, and the bleakness of the flight gave way to the love and vibrant joy of my family. "I was beginning to worry you weren't on there. How was the flight, any problems?"

"No, none at all," Wayne replied.

"How are the children?" I asked my brother.

"They've been pretty good, but Kristin likes to agitate the boys, doesn't she?"

"It's nice to see that everything is normal."

"She really has dad wrapped around her little finger, all she has to do is flash that little smile of hers or turn on a little pout and she can get away with anything."

Wayne laughed at my brother's observations. I couldn't respond. I was too busy trying to hold back the tears.

The children were the first to greet us at the door with their hugs and kisses. Without being asked, they volunteered how good they were for grandma and grandpa.

My brother helped us take the bags upstairs and in no time at all we were all settled.

After a night's sleep, we headed for my parent's summer home. Everything had been planned: Games for the children, golfing, tennis, swimming, boating, and fishing. The day's events would be topped off by a magnificent fireworks display.

The children awoke all excited ready for the long trip. We were on the road only fifteen minutes when Kristin asked for the first time, "When are we going to get there?" Quietly I told her we had a rather long trip and it would be best if she just fell asleep, and I would wake her when we got there.

I remembered taking this trip when my parents first bought the piece of property. It was a pretty drive any time of the year, but my favorite was the Fall when nature's brilliance was absolutely unequalled. The air always smelled fresh and crisp, and a scent of the autumn spices filled the air. The bright reds, yellows, and oranges painted pictures as far as the eye could see. The roadside food stands were filled with the colorful wares of the season, bright red apples, orange pumpkins, and the shiny skinned, green, yellow, orange squash. No roadside stand would be complete without the bright colors of the Indian corn hanging in clusters from every corner and apple cider jugs stacked up along the shelves. Oh, how I loved it, but never again would I be able to see it. But then, how many autumns were just memories for most Floridians, anyway? I thought about how wonderful it was to have had sight than never to have had it at all.

My thoughts focused on today: the sights that my children were seeing now. I knew the trees were lush and green and the corn in the fields should be about six feet tall. My father stopped at one of the roadside stands for a watermelon and a dozen ears of sweet corn. As usual, my father always knew the best place.

The car stopped again, and I could feel the familiar slope of my parents' driveway. The house was at the top of the hill, and the back yard sloped down to the lake. There was a small sandy beach where the edge of the property met the lake. My father's dock jetted out in a U-shape where he kept his boat. Shawn helped me inside where the surroundings were vaguely familiar. I had never seen the house completed. They were just finishing it when we moved to Florida. I remembered coming out to help them with the inside construction, staining the wood, and putting down the tiles in the bathroom floors. My mother gave me a full description of the interior decorating. I walked down the four steps into the family room and over to the sliding glass doors, unlocked them and walked outside, and stood on the back patio. I could hear the roar of the engines of the boats on the lake as they went zipping by.

"Look, Marc, look at the water skiers!" Shawn said to his brother loud enough for me to hear.

"That guy is on one ski," Marc responded.

The boys were anxious to get down to the dock. I decided to lay down the ground rules immediately. "No one, absolutely no one goes down to the dock without your father, grandpa, or grandma going with you. Do you understand?" I did not hear an acknowledgement. "I assume you both nodded your heads."

"Oh, yes, mom, we heard you," replied Shawn.

"Me, too, mom, we understand, no going down to the dock unless somebody goes with us," acknowledged Marc.

I heard them both go running inside as they slammed the sliding glass doors, screaming, asking grandpa if he wanted to go down to the dock and go fishing.

I went back inside and asked Wayne to bring the suit cases upstairs. My mother told me that we could have the back bedroom, the one that faced the lake. She knew I liked it best.

As I started unpacking, Kristin came running into the room, "Mommy, where's my bathing suit. Grandma said she would take me down to the lake and I could play in the sand and go in the water. Can I mom?"

"If grandma said she will go with you, yes." I found her bathing suit and helped her change. She gave me a kiss on the cheek and was gone. I heard her yelling as she ran down the steps. "Here I come, grandma, let's go." I walked over to the window and opened it wide. The breeze was cool off the lake. I could hear voices on the dock below. Wayne, Shawn, Marc, and my father had all gone fishing. Kristin was laughing, and playing with my mother. It all made for such a beautiful picture, one that I could see in my mind. I finished unpacking and went downstairs to sit out on the patio. I heard Wayne's voice, "Hey, look at that."

"Look, grandpa, look what I caught."

I heard my father's familiar laugh. It was the same laugh as when I had caught my first fish in Lake Erie. I was only Shawn's age the first time he took me fishing, and I remembered that first fish. It was a Sheepshead, only a couple of pounds. For me, at ten years old, it put up a good fight. I drifted from my thoughts back to the reality of my father's familiar laugh.

He spoke up loud and clear, as if he were reading my mind, "Hey, Sharon, it's about the size of your first one." How could he have known?

It was starting to get a little cool. I could tell the sun was going down. The family came into the house to fix dinner, watch T.V., and play some Uno. There was no argument tonight about getting ready for bed, even from Kristin. Everyone was tired from the fresh air. Tomorrow was to be the big day, and they all knew it. Some relatives had been invited out to Apple Valley to join in the festivities. We were all looking forward to it.

The children were up early. The aroma of the coffee, bacon, eggs, and toast reached the bedrooms. Through the open window I heard my father's voice with Shawn and Marc's at the dock getting some fishing in before breakfast. Quietly I slipped out of the bedroom to wash and dress.

"Good morning, mommy, I'm helping grandma," Kristin announced as I walked down the steps leading to the dining room. "You sit right here, mom," she said to me as she reached for my hand and placed it on the back of the chair where she wanted me to sit. I listened to my daughter as she continued to help my mother set the breakfast table.

"Marc caught a Blue Gill, it's a pretty nice sized one, too," my father said. Marc came in sloshing the pail filled with water and his Blue Gill. My mother told him that the fish had to stay outside on the patio. Kristin quickly dropped everything she was doing to run outside and inspect her brother's catch. Marc's fish seemed to be the highlight of the morning. I called the children inside, told the boys to wash their hands, and reminded them to use soap, as well as water.

My mother buttered my toast and made my tea. She had finally realized that I could manage to help myself and offered only this minor assistance. The conversation at this morning's breakfast table no longer focused on moving back to Ohio from Florida, the night of the attack, or even the events that would take place when we returned to Florida. It was the normal family conversation. Mother said the relatives would start arriving some time after noon and my brother Rick was expected any minute.

The boys helped my mother clear the breakfast dishes from the table. She insisted that I sit, relax, and have another cup of tea. My father took Wayne and the children for a boat ride on the lake. My mother and I decided to relax on the back patio. "Well, Sharon, how are things really going? I know you, you seem to be doing just fine. But what about Wayne, he seems so quiet."

Wayne was always quiet around my parents. However, there was more to it now. I didn't want my mother to worry. "I think he is going to be okay. Things seem a little bit strange right now, mom, but I think it's just going to take time."

"Be realistic, Sharon, this whole thing was rough for everybody, especially for you. We all went through it together. But, let's be serious, you were so independent before, and now whether you want to admit it or not, you are going to need some help. He always depended on you in the past, whether you could see it or not, and now, will you be able to depend on him? You know I worry about you, I guess mothers never stop worrying. I just want you to understand that I only want what is best for you."

I appreciated my mother's bluntness. I expected nothing less from her. I could not give her a definite answer about Wayne, because I just did not know. I could not read his mind, and he did not always share his innermost thoughts with me. His actions inside the house were not always what was best for me and the children, but I attributed this to the shock of what had happened. I did not want to think that it was out of a lack of concern, but rather out of a lack of enough time to make the adjustments to our new household situation. I wanted to believe that everything was going to work out. I knew there were no guarantees, and that his actions would be the proof of his ability or inability to accept what had happened. Only time would give me the answer. I prayed that I would recognize the course of action needed and have the wisdom and courage to follow it if the answer was negative.

"I don't know what to tell you, mom, I hope everything will be all right, but I just don't know. For now, everything is still a bit quiet. I know that the children are handling things all right, and speaking for myself, I know that I have adjusted. As for Wayne, there is just no way I can speak for him. I will just have to wait and find out."

I told my mother the doctor said the surgery was successful and my eye sockets had healed properly. There was no chance ever of restoring my sight. I told her that I would get plastic shells so I could open my eyes and have a natural appearance. I told her that I had one more major hurdle to overcome, the trial. There was no definite date set yet, but upon our return the depositions would be taken and the trial would be within the next few months. I told her of my reservations of getting on the witness stand and testifying for the State. I knew it was absolutely necessary, but it was not going to be easy.

"Do you want me to come down with you? I could stay there for the trial.'

I thought it would be best if she just stayed in Ohio. I told her that I would let her know the outcome.

"Somebody's here," I told my mother.

"I didn't hear anything."

"Where is everybody?" my brother Rick yelled from inside the house. "I had a feeling you two would be out here. Where's dad and the kids?"

"They all went for a ride on the boat. Rick, what time is it?"

"It's just a little after twelve, mom."

"I'd better get inside, I want to get some things ready for the cookout. Aunt Stel and Uncle Ed are supposed to be here around one."

"Do you need any help, Mom?" I asked her.

"No, just stay here, relax, I can manage."

I heard my mother get up and the sliding glass doors open. I heard my brother sit down in the place where my mother had been. My brother and I talked mostly about his interests. He told me about his band's prospects and plans. He wanted to take me to one of their practices so I could hear them. He talked about Florida and wondered if I was going to move back to Ohio. I told him I wasn't quite sure. Then he asked if we decided not to move if he could come down to visit during Spring break. I knew he had an ulterior motive in his line of questioning. Rick and I were always able to talk whether it be music, school, girl troubles, or the frustrations of living at home with my parents. Since I am six and a half years older, I guess that he felt I could give him some insight to solutions to some of the problems he faced.

"You know, Sharon, you don't act any different. Mom told everyone that you were doing okay, but we just thought it was the way she wanted to see things. It's kind of hard when you don't see it for yourself. I really didn't know what to expect. I didn't know if you were going to jump at every noise you heard, or be depressed, or even walk around crying all the time. I just didn't know. But mom was right, you are doing fine. I can see it for myself."

My brother and I sat quietly for only a few moments when I heard my father's boat approaching. "Dad's back."

"You're right, I better get down and help him tie the boat up to the dock." I heard my brother get up and leave and run down the hill.

I figured it was about time to go in and help my mother and show her exactly how proficient I had become around the kitchen. I helped her dice, chop, peel and mix. I think she was a little surprised at how well I had adapted to being unsighted. I was not as helpless as she had thought. My brother in his conversation had just confirmed what I had known all along, "Actions speak louder than words." If I didn't show her what I could do, how would she ever know?

The relatives arrived. My Aunt Stel, Uncle Ed, with my cousin Linda, her husband and their little daughter. A little later my Aunt Evelyn and Uncle Ray, my cousin, his wife, and their little boy all arrived. Each person identified her or himself by name, not realizing that I was able to tell them by their voices. They all sounded the same as I had recalled. They all were full of news. The occasion was pleasant.

"Remember the Fourth of July celebrations over at grandma's house?" my cousin Ray asked.

"You always brought enough fireworks to light up the whole street, you used to drive the neighbors crazy." My cousin informed me that he really hadn't changed that much and just like every other Fourth of July in the past, he had fireworks with him again.

The hours passed quickly, and the late afternoon turned into dusk and the dusk into night. I could not see it coming, but my children let me know that it was very much here by asking me, "When are the fireworks going to start?" My mother was standing by close enough to hear their questions, "You have about five more minutes, they start at ten o'clock. Go outside on the patio and get your seats. They are going to be shooting the fireworks display off over the lake."

"Mommy, I want to sit with you," Kristin said as she reached for my hand leading me to the outside. Wayne took the boys further down the hill away from the smaller children and broke open a package of sparklers. I hollered down in my motherly fashion to be careful, and they hollered back the usual, "We know." As expected my cousin set off his arsenal of Roman Candles, Bottle Rockets, M80s, Hammerheads and Cherry Bombs. I sat quietly listening to every blast and recalling how it used to be. And then, far off in the distance I heard the first crackle and explosion from the professional display. I could hear the "oohs" and "aahs" from the gathered friends and relatives. I could even smell the gunpowder. But there was something definitely missing when I could not see the burst of colors in the air. I sat there with Kristin on my lap with my face pointed toward the direction of the sounds. With closed eyes I strained to see. I wanted to ask was it blue, or red, or green? Was it the kind that filled the air that looked like a large chrysanthemum? I wanted to know, but everybody was busy watching. I felt left out, terribly isolated in my darkened world. I swallowed and tried to blink back the tears, but they started to flow freely. But I didn't mind, I knew that no one could see me in the darkness; besides, they were all too busy watching the display. I wrapped my arms around my daughter and squeezed her a little tighter. Quietly she whispered in my ear, "Mommy, that one was so pretty. It had blue and red and gold." It was as if she had known. She then reached for my hand; she held it flat in front of her and with her finger she drew what each firework looked like. "Mom, that one filled up the whole sky. It looked like it was going to fall down on us, too." How beautiful I thought. I'd seen firework displays repeatedly throughout my life, but now I was seeing them through the eyes of my little daughter. She continued describing each one in her soft, quiet voice. When the fireworks were shot off in rapid-fire succession, I knew it was time for the grand finale. She could no longer describe each one on my hand individually. They were coming too fast. The more they exploded, the louder she became. Her excitement grew and she jumped off my lap yelling, trying to keep her voice above the loud bursts from the fireworks. "Blue! Red! Gold! Green! The flower kind, the squiggly kind, the rainy kind!" My cousin's daughter joined in the excitement, hollering out each color as it appeared. I sat there laughing and so did everyone else. The visual splendor was being transmitted orally through the excitement of the children. I had my own personal firework display, and it would be one I would never forget.

The rest of the week was spent quietly at my parents' house. Once again I was waited on, no dishes to wash, no housecleaning to do. Even the children were taken care of. I spent some time visiting old friends. With each new reacquaintance of friends or relatives, there was a common course of interaction. I could feel the questions going through their minds. I imagined they all had preconceptions about how I would look and act. Everyone seemed to put her or himself in my situation. Meetings started out pretty much the same. First there was a sigh of relief that I was not disfigured. This was much to their surprise. No one really knew what I would look like after being shot in the head, but everybody imagined the worst. Next, it seemed as though they felt the topic of the attack was strictly off limits. They were relieved when they found they could talk about it openly and freely. Most of the time the conversation circumvented the issue. Then seemingly, out of curiosity, the questioning would hit the main target of the attack. Once the curiosity was satisfied and the awkwardness of the initial meeting had passed, we were all able to get on with more normal conversation.

The Fourth of July and the visits with old friends contrasted happily with our other major event for this vacation: A combined birthday party for all three children thrown by Wayne's sister. The children were not around for their birthdays, so this event was planned to give them a sense of occasion with Wayne's family. She had invited all of Wayne's relatives. Naturally the children were very excited, and so was I. I really like parties and family get-togethers.

I had never seen Wayne's sister's new house. Therefore, I was totally unfamiliar with the floor plan. Wayne led me inside and up the steps and over to the kitchen and then sat me at the kitchen table. Kristin sat down in the chair next to me. The boys, on the other hand, immediately left with Wayne's nephew, Jackie. Wayne's sister Joanne asked him if he would like to see the rest of the house. He told me just to sit, and he would be right back. Kristin was excited by the surrounding sights. She told me about the cakes on the kitchen table. She told me that there were two, and she knew just which one was hers. She first described the boys'. There were Darth Vader, R2D2, and C3PO. She took my hand to feel the next cake. "Be very careful, mom, just touch the hair and the face, don't go down any further because it's all frosting." She guided my hands gently over the head of the doll. "It's really pretty, gee I wish you could see it. She has blond hair, with blue eyes. Her dress is all frosting, I think the cake is underneath. The frosting is all white with pink flowers. She looks just like Cinderella." She sat on my lap informing me there were plenty of presents around and confessed that she couldn't wait to open them. "Does this mean I'm going to be four now?"

"No, Kristin, you are still only three and a half, but Aunty Joanne wasn't there for your third birthday, or for Shawn and Marc's either, so we're going to celebrate your birthday parties today."

Kristin naturally was overjoyed, after all, you can never have too many birthday parties—at least at her age.

Wayne's relatives began to arrive. Before long, the house was filled with familiar voices.

"Mom, Aunty Joanne wants to know if you would like a coke?" I expected to hear Shawn's footsteps run off to give Joanne my reply, instead, he turned around and said, "Yes, she wants one." Shawn then informed me that he was going to play. I heard his footsteps leave.

Once again I sat there alone quietly, listening to the voices that surrounded me. Occasionally I would hear a, "Hi," or Hello," and it sounded as though the word was directed to me. I'd respond with a hello, how are you, and wait for a reply, but there was none. It was then that I felt a little embarrassed at the possibility that that greeting was not directed towards me. As time passed, I became increasingly uncomfortable.

"Mom, is there anything you would like?" It was Marc this time checking up on me. "Whose coke is this on the table?"

"I guess it's mine," I told him. I had not even realized it was placed in front of me. I was never told.

The time was going by so slowly. I just sat there, listening. Kristin came over with Wayne's cousin's daughter, a little girl she had never met before. Kristin made the introduction, "This is my mom, but she can't see you, so if she asks you something, you can't shake your head, you have to answer her by talking." I couldn't help being amused by my daughter's explanation. They both sat down next to me and we carried on a delightful discussion. I pulled out the little micro-mini cassette recorder I had tucked away in my purse. I started to tape the chatter that was going on around us and then played it back to the girls. I asked if they knew any songs and I found out that they had both learned some of the same songs in preschool. We had our own little party, a time for fun, in recording their little songs and then playing them back. I heard Joanne's voice from out of the background, "Kristin, ask your mom if she would like us to sing happy birthday now."

"Mom, Aunty Joanne wants to know..."

"It's okay with me Kristin."

"Mom said it's okay with her Aunty Joanne." I couldn't help wondering why the question could not be directed to me. I was blind, not deaf.

Kristin wanted me to record this moment of excitement, the happy birthday song, so she could play it over and over again when we got back to Florida. I had captured everything on tape, even Kristin blowing out her candles. I left the recorder running while the children opened their presents amid background chatter and their screams of excitement. I shut the recorder off and slid it back into my purse. The party dispersed and moved to other rooms, some to the family room, some to the living room. I sat alone in the kitchen. I wondered what had happened. I tried to figure it out. I felt so isolated, so totally alone. I tried to find the reason. I knew from previous experiences of the initial awkward phase when I became reacquainted with people. Somehow, this time, it never got passed. No one even gave me the chance to talk. I didn't expect everyone to treat me as my own family did, but I never expected to be ignored.

I listened to see if I could pick up Wayne's voice. I heard Shawn the closest to me, "Shawn, could you come here, please?"

I heard his footsteps approach, "What do you want, mom?

"Could you take me to your father, please?" Shawn dropped me off near Wayne and then left. Wayne was standing talking to his uncle. As soon as I came, his uncle left.

I reminded Wayne that we needed to leave soon.

Wayne moved me to a chair in another room and told me that we would be leaving shortly. Once again I was left alone, sitting quietly, listening to the children play video games on the television set. I felt so confined. I hated feeling confined. I had no idea where I was. These new surroundings were confusing. I did not want to be a nuisance or a bother, so I sat back in the chair listening to the video game, and just waited, impatiently, until it was time for us to leave.

Joanne told Wayne how wonderful it was to see him and the children again and how glad she was that we could make it out there. We thanked her for her hospitality, and Wayne led me to the car. I was quiet on the way home, I really didn't know what to say. I tried to sort through the whole experience. I was feeling things I had never felt before, anger, frustration, loneliness, and in general terribly disturbed by the whole evening. Wayne broke the ice with the first question, "Well, Sharon, did you have a good time?" I could not tell if he was being sarcastic or not. He had to be kidding, I thought.

"Joanne's house is really nice. It's big, isn't it?"

"I really wouldn't know, I did not get the chance to see the whole house."

"Well, there is no reason for me to have to take you around anyhow. You wouldn't be able to see the house anyway." That comment hurt, and coming from my own husband, it was not a good sign.

I would have liked to believe that he was attempting humor, but pretending has never been one of my strong suits. Increasingly, I was getting the feeling that he was embarrassed to have me around. *"Ten and a half years, that's quite a while. We have been through rough times before, but not as rough as this."*

"I never realized how much I needed you." I kept thinking of his words. Did he feel that he needed me so much before with sight but that he no longer needed me now without sight? What was going to happen to us now? Was our marriage based on that much need and that little love? Was that bond holding us together necessity rather than strong love that holds people together "for better or worse, in sickness and in health...?"

We were only a couple of days away from the end of our vacation. We had to get back home and try to steer our life back on a normal heading. It had been nearly two months since the attack. I still had the trial to face. I wondered what "normal" would mean for us and when we would find it.

CHAPTER SIX
Trial

When we returned from vacation in the middle of July, I had to face the prospect that the trial would come soon. It was easy to say in the emergency room that I wanted to prosecute. It was going to be more difficult steeling myself to be the chief witness for the prosecution.

I had heard stories of women who were terrified to testify in a rape case for fear of retaliation, for fear of humiliation, and even for fear of accusation that they might have contributed to the crime by encouraging the rapist in some way. I was not going to be deterred. I needed this man off the streets forever. He had rendered me blind and defenseless. If he came again, I had no way of preventing a repeat of the events of May 23rd. So I called the State Attorney's office to arrange to do my part. The prosecutor, Mr. Garfield, informed me that he would make arrangments for both Wayne and me to give depositions. Wayne's testimony was needed on some of the physical evidence.

After hanging up the phone, I thought about that man sitting in prison, the faceless man that struck out of the darkness. I couldn't help wondering where he came from, who he was, and why, why he chose me. The police had already told me that I was singled out by random, that the man had seen me driving down the road as he was pulling out of a parking lot. He decided to follow me. They also had told me that he had done this before, and in police talk, his M.O. was to disable his victim first, return, offer assistance, and then stab and rape his victim. If he had done this before, why was he allowed to be on the streets where he could do this to me? What could possibly make a human being strike out and terrorize another fellow human being in such a fashion? Where did the whole thing start—someplace in his childhood? How could it have been prevented? Wasn't there someone who could have seen the violence and the potential danger of letting this man out? Then I thought about the police. The detectives who investigated my case were homicide detectives. How many times had they seen crimes similar to mine where the victims died? How did they feel when they apprehended a criminal like this one, who had been freed after committing a similar crime? How terribly frustrating. I was sure they read him all his rights as required by the Miranda Decision. I'm sure they obtained all the proper search warrants they had to. I'm sure that every detail was documented properly. I remembered my examination, to prosecute for the rape. I remembered that everything had to be documented and witnessed in order to be admissible in court. I knew that our legal system protected the rights of the criminal. Everybody involved in law enforcement on my case had to be very careful not to violate those precious rights. I couldn't help feeling a little angry toward the system. I know that being a citizen of the United States guarantees every human certain rights specified in the Constitution of the United States. That is what makes us such a great country; those rights are preserved and protected. The rights of the criminal in my case were preserved by the Constitution. I couldn't help thinking about me, the victim, on the other side of the fence. Who was out there to guarantee my rights? That criminal did not read me my rights and consider that I had the right to life before he pulled the trigger and tried to take my life, again when he tried to suffocate me with the pillow, and then a third time when he pushed the knife into my chest. I did not hear anything about my rights. It was not just my life that had been affected. I was not the only victim. What about my children? They were also victims. I came so close to being taken away from them forever. I had returned to them in a way which I never expected to return. I would never see them again. And my loss of sight would be a continuous reminder to them as well as to me of that horrible night. My parents were victimized and so was my husband, Wayne. I found the list of victims growing. What about all the taxpayers who would have to pay to bring him to trial again, and if he were found guilty, who would be supporting him while in prison?

A senseless act of violence committed by the hand of one person could disrupt and change forever the lives of so many. The criminal's rights were protected and guaranteed by law. My rights had not been protected and guaranteed!

I found some comfort in thinking that I was fortunate to live in the State of Florida where we had a Crimes Compensation Act to provide for a victim. I knew that all the formalities and the paperwork had been completed. The woman from the Crimes Compensation Bureau in Fort Lauderdale had told Wayne and me not to worry, that she felt in view of the heinousness of the crime, there would be no difficulty in securing the maximum amount from the Crimes Compensation Bureau in Tallahassee. After all, that's what they were there for, to compensate victims of crime. I had lost my earning capacity, at least within the confines of the career that I had. My desk was cleared out before I was released from the hospital, but that was not unusual. After all, I needed to see in order to hold that type of job. I depended on sight to look at the smashed cars. I also depended on the mobility, the use of a car. What good was a blind adjuster? And at my company, especially, I was of absolutely no use to them any longer. I was surprised that I was not given an exit interview as were most other employees upon their separation from the company.

The loss of my income was devastating. We had just purchased the house based on two incomes. It was definitely going to hurt. I decided to make a quick call to Social Security to find out how my claim was progressing. I was advised that I would not receive my first check until five months had passed. This was to guarantee that I was totally disabled. I was informed that the amount would be $450 a month which also included my allotment for my three minor children. I thought that the amount sounded low since it included the amount for the three children as well. The voice on the other end told me if I had been shot prior to January of 1979, the amount would have been much more, close to double. I apologized for not having better timing and thanked her for the information.

When the time came for the depositions, Wayne and I went to the prosecuting attorney's office. There we met the prosecutor for the first time, and the Public Defender who would be representing my attacker. Outside of his office everything was warm and cordial, but inside it was down to business. I was first to give my deposition while Wayne waited in the outer office. Mr. Garfield, the prosecutor for the State, sat to my right. The Public Defender sat directly across the desk from me. At first his voice sounded a bit uneasy. He started his line of questioning with the beginning of that night, where I was, who I was with, and what I was doing. He continued on through the attack. He even asked if I went with the man willingly. I knew that was coming. He had me recap every detail of the events of that night, as painful as they were. I felt strong and kept on going. It was not difficult to bring forward the words. I felt so confident. We were in there an hour, but it seemed like only moments. I stood up to leave and my knees were not as strong as usual. Mr. Garfield helped me to the waiting room and told Wayne that he would be next. I stood for a moment and felt dizzy. Voices started to become distant, and I felt faint. Quickly I sat down and asked for a glass of water. I felt so strong in that room. I felt confident and self-assured, but now, after it was all over, I was totally drained and terribly weak. *"My God, would I make it through the trial?"*

Wayne returned very soon. Rick advised us that he would call us if we were needed for anything else. He told me that he would keep me informed as to what was going on, and that the trial had been set for some time in late October.

I was still weak walking to the car, and the ride home was very quiet. Wayne had very little to say, and I did not feel like a conversation. My thoughts turned to my reaction to the deposition. I thought for sure that I would have been able to handle it better than I did. According to Mr. Garfield, I was just fine. Maybe I was just fine in there, but I was a nervous wreck now. I kept wondering about the trial, when I would be in the same room with my attacker once again. How was I going to feel just knowing he was sitting out there watching every move that I made? And just as during that night, I would not be able to see him. I tried to calm myself and reason myself into regaining my composure. I knew I had to be calm, and once the trial was over I could then place the horrible nightmare right where it belonged, as part of my past—if they got the horrible man off the streets.

The trial began two days before Halloween. My attacker had already performed his trick and had his treat. I hoped that this Halloween the decent people would do something about at least one ghoul. I had done everything I could to prepare, from the less than dignified gathering of evidence from my body to the giving of depositions, and to going over the events repeatedly in my mind so I would be sure of my statements. I felt I was mentally prepared. But being mentally prepared and going through the actual physical experience are two different things.

The children were already dressed and ready to go. "Good luck, mom," said Shawn as he walked out the door.

"Try not to be too nervous, mom, good luck," added Marc. I hurried my dressing so Wayne and I could beat the morning rush-hour traffic. This morning we drove Kristin to the day care center where we picked up an additional passenger. One of the young women who was working the morning that Wayne came and told them that I was missing wanted to attend the trial. I felt there would be no harm in letting Trina come along. After all, I could use the additional support.

The morning traffic on the interstate was busy. Conversation within our car was confined to the traffic and the weather, things people normally talk about when they don't know what else to say. Parking around the courthouse was always a problem, but in our case, a space had been reserved. The sign in front said, "Handicapped Parking Only." We rushed into the courthouse and took the elevator up to the third floor. The elevator doors opened. I reached out for Wayne's arm grasping it firmly and tiptoeing over the threshold so not to catch my heel in the crack of the elevator door. We walked down the hallway and were greeted by Mr. Garfield. "The jury selection has been completed and we will be ready to start in about ten minutes."

He ushered us to a single row of benches in front of the courtroom doors. "You can just sit here and relax, I'll let you know when we're about to begin."

I turned toward Trina, "Relax, easy for him to say."

The hallway in front of me was filled with sounds of confusion. Footsteps raced back and forth. Voices of every pitch and tone filled the corridor. Rick's voice sounded. "We're ready to start. There are some motions that need to be addressed and then will come the opening arguments. I'm then going to start calling witnesses. First will be Charlie Greenwood and next the woman who lived across the street who also saw you screaming on the balcony, then will be the owner of the property and fourth will be Tammy. When you hear Tammy leave and go inside the courtroom, prepare yourself because you'll be next. I will send the bailiff, Al, out to walk you into the courtroom. I will be seated off to your right down in front."

I heard the click of his cowboy boots fade down the hall. The sounds of confusion and loud voices were now muffled behind the courtroom doors. A hush fell over the few voices remaining in the corridor.

I thought about the witnesses who were to precede me. I did not realize that a woman saw me screaming on the balcony. Why didn't she come to my aid? Tammy, my brother's girlfriend at the time, was the reason I was in Ft. Lauderdale that fateful night. I was sure that she would never forget the experience: First the phone call in the middle of the night inquiring about my whereabouts and now the appearance on the witness stand as the last person to be with me before the attack.

"Stay calm. Take a deep breath. Everything is going to be all right. Relax," I muttered softly to myself. These were all the things my mother would say to me if she were here. I could hear Wayne's footsteps pacing back and forth in front of me; I wanted to do the same. Trina placed her hand on mine and give them a slight pat. She didn't have to say anything because there was really nothing left to be said. I heard the courtroom doors open again, "I'm next," came the familiar tone of Tammy's voice as she walked towards the doors.

"Now, I'm next." It seemed like only a few moments had passed when the doors opened again. This time it should have been for me, but I heard the familiar click of Rick's boots. He told me that Al, the bailiff, was going to come for me. "What are you doing here?" I directed my comment to where I thought his face would be.

"The defense counsel objected to the bailiff walking you in. They wanted me to do it. I don't know why. They just objected."

I gave Trina my purse and stood up, straightening my jacket and skirt. "Do you have your cane with you?" It was half a question, half demand, "Yes."

"Well, I would like you to use it."

I pulled the folding cane out of my purse and opened it. I placed the cane in my left hand and reached for Rick's arm with my right. Wayne was silent as he opened the doors to the courtroom. Rick paused for only a moment before walking down the aisle. All was completely silent. It was eerie not having any sounds by which to gauge myself.

"Are you ready, here we go," Rick whispered to me as he started walking down the aisle. I had a feeling all eyes were on me, and I did not need a verbal confirmation from anyone. Very cautiously and slowly he walked me down the aisle to the witness stand. There I received help from the bailiff and the clerk.

The bailiff took my cane and adjusted the microphone for me. The judge asked me if I was ready to begin. I cleared my voice and said, "Yes, I am." The words came out so weak and faint he could barely hear me. "Would you please speak up, Mrs. Komlos." My God, I thought, this is it, this is really it. I could feel my hands trembling so I placed them in my lap, perhaps removing them from the view of all those who were watching. I knew the jury was to my right, and my attacker, whose name was Rossi, was to my left in front. It was frightening to know that he was out there somewhere in the darkness. I could hear no movement coming from the defense table, but he was there. I felt a cold chill go down my spine, anticipating the inevitable. I had to go through it one more time, every detail. I would have to answer the questions as they were asked and be careful not to give too much and not to give too little. I found little comfort in knowing that it had to be done. I wanted to scream, just yell at him, "Why? What in God's name ever possessed you to do such a bizarre thing?" I wondered if he realized the impact it had on my family. Could he ever know what it was like? How my three children felt? Did he know what it felt like to be blind? And there he sat, quietly, watching.

There was complete silence in the courtroom. The room seemed so vast with its high ceilings that even a whisper would echo. I knew that every word I was about to speak would be heavily weighed by those faceless people who filled the void in front of me.

"Would you please give us your full name."

"Sharon Marie Komlos," I said softly.

"I am going to ask that you speak slowly, please, and the jury is about at a thirty degree angle to your right," Mr. Garfield said in a stern tone.

"Okay."

"Look in their general direction. How old are you please?"

I turned my head to the right as he had instructed, "Thirty one," I said more loudly.

"What is your occupation?"

"My previous occupation was in insurance, Outside Claims Adjuster."

"Where do you reside at the present time?" I gave him my address. "What type of place is that?" I told him that it was a single family home.

Judge Kaplan interrupted, "Excuse me, can everybody hear her?"

I could hear the response from the voices off to my right, "Not too well." I knew that my voice was soft, but I thought that they could all hear me. I was still very nervous and did not want them to hear that.

"The jury is at about a thirty-five degree angle to your right, but the microphone is right in front of you. You are probably better off speaking right in front of you. Try moving the chair up a little closer."

The judge then instructed the clerk, "Mr. Spina, push the chair a little closer. Just look in front of you, you don't have to look at the jury. Mr. Garfield is in front of you."

I reached out to touch the microphone, to make sure it was directly in front of me. Once again I placed my hands back on my lap. Mr. Garfield continued where he had left off. Now my voice echoed throughout the courtroom.

"Can you give us a brief account of what you did on the evening of May 22, 1980?"

I retold the horrors of the night in great detail.

All they wanted to hear was the story until I entered the hospital. The pain and suffering and surgery and deprivation and lost job and lost income and frustration and extra effort and injuries to my family were not part of my story in the criminal justice system. As soon as we had me in surgery, Mr. Garfield turned to the question of criminal insanity. The test in Florida is whether the criminal knew right from wrong. Rossi certainly had known that.

"Do you recall anything about the manner in which Mr. Rossi spoke to you, his speech patterns?"

"There was nothing unusual. It was unslurred. It was coherent."

"Just answer the following two questions with a yes or no," Rick said.

"Judge," Bernard Walsh objected, "Before we go any further, I renew my motion to exclude this testimony."

"May we approach the bench, Your Honor?" Mr. Garfield asked. I heard Mr. Walsh and Mr. Garfield walk up to the front of Judge Kaplan. I heard them discussing heatedly something about the testimony to be inadmissible. Judge Kaplan then dismissed the jury and requested that the prosecuting attorney and public defender join him in his chambers for a few moments.

"Your Honor, would it be possible for Mrs. Komlos to get down from the witness stand while we adjourn to your chambers? I think she would feel better if she were not sitting up here all alone." I was grateful that Mr. Garfield made his request. I shuttered at the thought that I would be left on display on the witness stand with no jury, no judge, no prosecutor or defense counsel, but just the eyes of Mr. Rossi staring at me. Mr. Garfield helped me down off the witness stand and then turned me over to the waiting hands of Trina who walked me down the center aisle that splits the defense from the prosecution. We sat down together in one of the benches near the rear of the courtroom.

"He didn't even have the nerve to look at you, Sharon," Trina said softly. "As you walked past he tried to look back at you, but he kept his head down low and just turned his head a little, not even enough to look up at your face."

"What is he wearing? Is his hair still long? Did he show any signs of reaction when I was talking?" I whispered to Trina.

"He just sits there with a somber look on his face, very quiet, staring down at a paper cup on the table in front of him. He's wearing a rust-colored suit and his hair is cut short. He looks like any normal guy you'd see on the street. He's showing no reaction whatsoever. He just keeps his head down most of the time."

I sat quietly, and I wondered if he was as terrified now as I was when my fate was in his hands.

I heard the judge's chamber doors open. Once again they were about to begin. Trina led me back to the witness stand where the bailiff helped me back to the chair and adjusted the microphone. Judge Kaplan advised me that I was still under oath. There was first some discussion before the jury returned, but then they were brought back and Mr. Garfield continued with his line of questioning.

"Mrs. Komlos, would you please answer the following questions with just a yes or no answer."

"Do you have an opinion as to whether this individual was able to understand the nature and quality of his actions or their consequences?"

"Yes, I do."

"Do you have an opinion as to whether or not this individual was capable of distinguishing that which is right from that which is wrong, and both of those questions go from the time that you first encountered him to the time that you no longer were in his presence."

"Yes."

"What is your opinion as to whether or not he was able to understand the nature and quality of his actions or their consequences?"

"Yes, he definitely knew."

"What is your opinion as to whether or not he was able to distinguish that which is right from that which is wrong?"

"Yes, he definitely knew the difference between right and wrong."

"Now, I'd like to ask you to tell the jury the underlying reasons for your opinions."

"Starting right from the beginning of the incident, the way he so hurriedly grabbed me and threw me onto the back floor of the car so that nobody could see me, and the way he told me to keep down, and the way he did obey all the traffic laws—he definitely knew the difference between right and wrong.

"He did not go through a red light, and, finally, when we got into the apartment, when he was smothering me with a pillow and I screamed at him that he was suffocating me and I couldn't breathe, he took it off and said oh, he was sorry."

"I have no further questions of this witness," said Rick Garfield.

"Sharon, came the voice, "I'm Bernie Walsh. I think you recognize my voice because we talked before. I have a few questions for you, Sharon.

"One of them refers to after the pillow incident. You finally pushed him off and you said, 'Wait, wait a minute, you're smothering me,' and he responded, 'Oh, I'm sorry,' and then he took the pillow away.

"That was an abrupt action on his part, an abrupt change in mood; is that right, from smothering you to stopping like that?"

"Well—"

"Is that how you recall it?"

"First of all, I did not push him off...He took it off. I can't say it was really abrupt. He just laid it aside and took it off."

"Sharon," Walsh continued, "during this incident, later, after the pillow struggle, after he was acting like your husband or whatever—somewhere in there—by that time, you felt like you were dealing with an irrational, crazy person; isn't that right?"

"Well," I said, "I do not know if he was trying to keep me calm or what by just pacifying me, and going along with me also."

"Sharon, do you recall ever taking a deposition with myself and the State Attorney, Mr. Garfield?"

"Yes, I do."

"Please think very carefully now. Do you recall me asking you a question outlining the above, and asking you that after the husband incident, and the pillow incident, that you figured you were dealing with an irrational, crazy person?

"Do you recall me asking you that question?"

"Yes, I do."

"Do you recall giving the answer to me of yes?"

"The answer was given yes . . . for a loss for any other words."

"Okay," said Bernie Walsh abruptly. "Thank you very much, Sharon."

"Just one question on redirect," Garfield asked.

"Back at that same deposition, which for the record was given on August 21, 1980, at 2:30 P.M. in my office, do you recall your answer as follows: 'I didn't say he was crazy. I said the person that did this is dangerous, that he had a gun, and I didn't know when he was coming back.' "

"Yes, I recall that."

"I have no further questions."

"Anything else, Mr. Walsh?" asked the Judge.

"No, Your Honor."

"All right," said Judge Kaplan. "Just hold on a second. We will get you off the stand."

I breathed a sigh of relief. Thank God it was over. Al came over to help me down off the witness stand. In dead silence I walked down the aisle holding onto Al's left arm. I could then hear the inaudible amplified voices through the partially opened courtroom doors, but when they slammed shut, silence again filled the outer hall.

"Well, how did everything go?" Wayne asked as he came forward to take over for Al.

"She held up like a trooper, she's really terrific." I thought Al was most kind with his comment. I was still trembling on the inside.

"Sharon, would you like something to drink? How about if I take you in the back room?"

Wayne told me that he would wait in the outer hall to talk to Rick Garfield. It was close to lunchtime, and they should be recessing soon. Al pointed Wayne to where he would be taking me. I heard nothing so I assumed Wayne nodded his head in acknowledgment.

"That guy ought to be hung by his —" I knew that Al was strictly expressing his own opinion. I could feel his anger coming through and I know that it was shared by many of my friends and relatives.

"You know we even had to frisk your husband when he came in here this morning, we're just too good to guys like these." Al took me to the back room and sat me down. He got me a glass of water and told me that the court would be recessing very shortly.

For lunch, Trina, Wayne, and I went upstairs to the coffee shop, which was naturally crowded during the afternoon lunch break. I went through the line with Wayne and ordered the safest thing possible. I figured they couldn't do much damage to a cheeseburger, french fries or a Coke. I handed the woman the money and waited for the change. Wayne simply placed my open palm directly under the hand of the cashier. I held onto my tray with one hand reaching for Wayne's arm with the other. He led me over to the closest open booth. "They're blind," he said quietly.

"So am I." Trina read to me the little sign posted near the cash register. It told everyone that the clerks were rehabilitated and provided by the Blind Services. I forgot that they told me I might be able to do this when they rehabilitated me. Somehow, I could not envision myself for the rest of my life being a clerk in the courtroom coffee house.

When we returned from lunch, Rick Garfield met us in the outer hall. "Mr. Komlos, I won't be needing you to testify. The defense counsel stipulated that everything you said would be true and since I was only going to have you identify the car and the personal effects of your wife, putting you on the stand would be unnecessary. There are a few other witnesses we won't be calling as well. They will all be dismissed."

"Mr. Garfield, would we be able to stay and listen to the testimony?" I asked.

"Somehow I had a feeling you were going to ask that question, so just to play it safe I asked Mr. Walsh if he had any objections to you being present. He did and the Court concurred with his objections. I could understand their position. With you being physically present in the courtroom, it could draw sympathy from the jury. That seems to be the only reason since I don't plan on recalling you as a witness. Mr. Komlos, however, can stay and listen if he would like to since the jury doesn't even know who he is and he will not be called to testify."

"I would like to be present for the reading of the verdict. Would that be possible?" I asked Rick.

"I'll check to be sure there are no objections. I don't think there will be, since the jury will have already made up their minds, but I'll let you know for sure."

I heard the bailiff in the background letting everyone know that Judge Kaplan was ready to reconvene.

"I have to get back now. By the way, Sharon, you were really terrific up there. You were bomb proof," I heard him say as he started walking towards the courtroom doors.

"Well, what would you like to do? Would you like to stay here or do you want to go home?" Wayne asked. Trina just stood silently by waiting for my response.

"Since I can't go in there, I have to sit out here on the bench. More than likely both of you would like to hear what will be going on. I really don't want to sit out here all alone. I would feel much more comfortable at home. Would you mind if we left now, I'm really rather tired? I would just like to go home and rest."

Trina was not going to interfere with our decision but admitted that she had to get back to work. There was no longer any reason why we could not discuss the trial, but discussing the trial was the last thing I wanted to do.

I was relieved that my part was concluded. I felt totally drained, and I was worried. A long list of witnesses still had to testify. I knew that there was plenty of physical evidence to bring in a guilty verdict on all the charges. There were two counts of attempted murder, one in the first degree and one in the second degree. There was one count of sexual battery, and one count of kidnapping. Mr. Rossi had even given a statement to the police, from what I was told previously, that he had committed the crimes. His plea was, "not guilty by reason of insanity," and I knew that this would be more difficult to prove. There was just no way to read the jury on something like this. It could go either way. I shuddered at the thought of Rossi back on the streets within a year or two after only spending a minimal amount of time in a mental institution.

"He knew what he was doing was wrong, I know he knew it. He knew he would be punished if caught," I said out loud as I pounded my fist on the seat next to me. "What if they don't believe me?"

I felt Wayne's hand reach over and pat me on my wrist, "Just try to relax, it's going to be all right." The words rang hollow; I knew I would not be able to relax until the verdict was read and his fate decided. Then, and only then, would I know if things were going to be all right. I knew I was going to have to prepare for whatever that final verdict was. I was going to have to accept it, like it or not. Then a chilling thought cut me, "You know something, Wayne, Rossi is just one man, I remember reading newspaper stories about people who committed crimes like him over and over again, he's not the only one out there. What about all the others?"

We dropped Trina off at the day care center, and I thanked her for being with me. As soon as we returned home I had to call my mother and give her a full report of the day's events.

"I'm just glad to hear that your testimony is over with," my mom responded when she heard my news.

"So am I, mom, so am I."

The second day of the trial was a lot worse for me than the first. It was not easy sitting home, alone, wondering what was going on in Broward County Courthouse. The house was so silent. I turned on the television hoping for some distraction. I went into the kitchen and decided to bake something for the children. I pulled out the bowls, the measuring cups, the spoons and found my mini tape recorder with the recipe. I paced back and forth in the kitchen not really knowing what I was looking for, not being able to keep my mind on what I was doing. I replaced the baking equipment. I sat in the kitchen for a while and tried to decide what I would prepare for dinner. I made a cup of tea and started playing recipes on my tape recorder. I finally decided that McDonalds would do just fine. Wayne could pick something up on his way home from the courthouse. I would give him the order when he called. I reached over for the telephone on the counter and picked it up to check if the line was working properly. We never had any difficulties with the telephone lines, but I just wanted to be sure.

I called Virginia at the day care center to talk for a few moments, but her time was cut short by an argument in the three-year old's room. The telephone rang, and I picked it up on the first ring. "Hello."

"May I speak with Helen, please?" the unfamiliar woman's voice asked.

"I'm sorry. You must have the wrong number." I made myself a cup of tea and went back into the living room to see if I could concentrate on one of the morning game shows. My thoughts drifted to yesterday.

I was surprised that the Public Defender did not ask me more questions. But he was only trying to establish that his client was insane. He questioned my use of "crazy." I remembered now, when I used that word. It was when Charlie came up to rescue me. I hope that fact was made clear enough to the jury that "crazy" was used for lack of a better word. Oh how I wanted to go back and reinforce that to them. I did not say "crazy," to mean "insane." I hoped that I didn't ruin the whole case for Mr. Garfield. The telephone rang again. "Hello."

"Hi, it's me. Are you all right?" Wayne asked.

"Yes, I just had to run to get the phone, I must have sounded out of breath."

"You sound like it. We just adjourned for lunch. The first person to testify this morning was Detective Haas. I tried to listen to most of his testimony, but when they played Rossi's statement, I just had to leave the courtroom. I just couldn't take it. I couldn't stand listening to his voice. I had a chance to talk to the young woman who this guy assaulted up in New York. We didn't know it yesterday, but she could not positively identify him in the courtroom. But something happened this morning. They were bringing him into the courtroom, and she met him in the hall. Seeing him that way, she was able to identify him immediately. He hit her with a car and then came back to offer her care. He raped her and stabbed her and left her for dead in a shallow grave. But she lived and gave enough information to get him convicted and sent to prison for ten years. He was paroled after seven years but got into trouble again, so he did another three years. There was some suspicion that he was responsible for killing some women in upstate New York, but there was not enough physical evidence to make an arrest." I sat back in my chair, stunned by what I was hearing. "I better get going now. I want to get something to eat before they start again. I'm not going to stay until the very end. I want to get out of here before rush-hour traffic starts."

"Will you call me before you start for home?" I asked him.

"Why?"

"The children should be home from school by then, and I can find out what they would like from McDonalds, you can pick it up on your way home."

"Let's go there instead, it will get you out of the house. I'll see you in a little while."

That evening, I told my mother about the day's events as they were relayed to me by Wayne. I poured out my heart on the telephone. I told her how difficult it was to believe that I was in the hands of a man who attacked that young woman in 1970 and who may have murdered those women in upstate New York. He was again in court being tried for the same type of crime. I told her how it's so ironic, the little twists and turns that life takes. How it can change in only seconds. I felt like my life was on hold awaiting the outcome of this man's fate. I looked at how much of my time he was occupying, and I didn't even know him. I didn't even know what he looked like or why he did it.

"Mom, you wouldn't believe it, sitting there in the restaurant, listening to the conversations going on around me. It was as if nothing had really changed yet everything had changed. Shawn, Kristin and Marc were still talking about school, arguing with each other, kicking each other under the table; there were people in the room talking about the trying day at work, of the traffic jam on Glades Road, and how a neighbor's friend had a baby just this morning."

Even after I finished the conversation with my mother and hung up the telephone, I couldn't help wondering "what happens if," what happens if his plea of insanity is believed and he gets off? What happens if he goes into a mental hospital and suddenly has a miraculous recovery? What happens if he's out on the streets within a short time, who will be his next victim? My feelings were very strong, and I had no doubt whatsoever that there would be another victim. Would she live or die? Would the police have enough evidence to tie him to the crime? Would the taxpayers pay once again to bring him to trial for the same crime? How many times would this happen? How could I ever feel safe with him on the loose?

I said good-night to the boys, gave each an extra hug and a kiss on the cheek, remembering how close I came to not even being here for them. I went into Kristin's room, tucked her in, kissed her good-night and gave her a hug.

"Mommy, are you worried about something?"

I guess I couldn't hide it from my daughter. I thought carefully before I answered her question. I didn't want to frighten her, but I wanted to be honest, "Well, just a little. But everything is going to be all right."

"I heard you talking to Daddy about the man who shot you, I know that he's in court. Is that why you are worried?" She paused for a few seconds and then continued, "Mommy, what's court?"

"Oh, sweetheart, court is a place where a person goes when he breaks the law and is arrested by the police. The room that he goes into is a big room in a place called the courthouse and a judge sits behind a big bench and there are people there called the jury. On one side of the room sits the person who committed the crime and the man or woman who is an attorney, the person that will be speaking for him to try and help him. On the other side of the room sits the person who was hurt by the other person. The person who was hurt has an attorney, too; he is the one who speaks for that person. And they sit all day or however long it is going to take and talk about what had happened. Each person gets to explain what happened and how it happened. And the other person tries to explain why he did it. It's rather complicated, and I'm not even sure if you understand what I'm trying to tell you, but it is very serious because if the people who sit and listen, the jury, think the person who broke the law really and truly did it, he can be put in jail for a long, long time."

"Is the man who shot you going to jail for a long time?"

"That is something we don't know right now. The whole thing is not over yet and that is the reason I am a little worried."

"Mommy, don't worry. The people who are listening, they will be able to tell that he did something bad to you and then they will make him go to jail for a long, long time. You always tell me that if people do something bad, they get punished. Just like when I do something bad, I get punished. They will know, mom, you watch, they will know that he did something bad and he has to be punished too."

"You'd better go to sleep now, Kris, it's getting late and you have to get up for school in the morning."

"I love you, mommy, don't worry. Everything will be all right."

I gave her another kiss and another hug. She was my own little pillar of strength, what an optimistic child-like view she had of the world around her.

I walked out of her room and turned off the light. I wished I could be as confident as she. There she was, almost four years old, and she knew the difference between right and wrong. She knew that when you did something wrong, you were punished. Even at her own young and tender age, she knew the difference between right and wrong, was so thoroughly convinced that he, too, knew the difference between right and wrong and that by doing something wrong, he would be punished. How could a four year old know the difference and a thirty-two year old man not? Oh, how I prayed that the jury would see this as well. These thoughts kept ringing in my head all night. Tomorrow would be the day, Wayne had said, when the doctors were to take the stand: Two for the State and two for the defendant. It was almost over. According to what he had said, tomorrow would be the last day of the testimony.

I wanted the whole thing to be finished.

The third day of the trial was Halloween, and it turned out to be the ghoul's best day in court. Once again, Wayne left the house early to fight the rush-hour traffic. I asked him if he would call me during every break. It was getting close to the end, and I wanted to know everything that was going on. I explained to him it was difficult sitting at home wondering what was going on.

After the children left, I decided to go and listen to a book in my room. It was the first tape I received from the Talking Books for the Blind.

"The Eye of a Needle," the male voice read aloud on the tape recorder. I listened to the tape intrigued by how the man's voice changed with every character he portrayed. It was like listening to television. I was able to imagine every movement the way it would be enacted. In this novel a stiletto is used by the Nazi spy. Instantly, it brought attention to my own wound. While listening to the tape, I touched the center of my chest and felt the scar. A stiletto plunged up into the heart of the victim—it was frightening to think about everything that could have happened. Thankfully the telephone interrupted the male voice on my recorder. Wayne was on the first break, but there was really no news. There were too many motions, arguments, and discussions at the bench. He would let me know more about the doctors' testimony at lunch break. I hung up the phone and depressed the keys of my tape recorder. The male voice continued.

It really did not bother me listening to the account of how the stiletto had been used. As I had always told my children if they watched something spooky or scary on television, it was only a story. I found myself to be more intrigued by the voice, the inflections and accents of the man reading the story. It was like listening to a play on a tape recorder. I took the tape recorder into the kitchen and made myself a cup of tea. I thought how interesting it was to be able to listen to a novel and make tea at the same time. And it was certainly a lot better than the day before when I waited for word without this diversion.

"I couldn't do this while reading a book in my sighted days," I said to myself. I carried the tape recorder back to the living room and sat down on my chair. I sipped tea and got lost in the intrigue of the German spy. It helped to pass the time until the next ringing of the telephone.

I was not surprised that it was Wayne. "Well, Sharon, it doesn't look too good. Two of the doctors for the defendant have taken the stand. Both testified that Rossi was insane at the time he committed the crime.

They appeared rather convincing. There are two doctors left to testify this afternoon, both for the State. Up to this point I would have said that we had the case locked up tight. There's plenty of evidence to convict him of the crime, but now I'm not so sure. The whole issue of insanity is rather touchy."

Wayne's words produced a sinking feeling in my stomach. I sat quietly, just listening. I didn't inquire any further. "When will you be coming home?"

"I would like to stay for the rest of the testimony. I'd like to hear what the doctors on the other side are going to say. It really shouldn't take too much longer. Mr. Garfield said that today is the last day of testimony, that the closing arguments and the jury deliberation will take place on Monday. Do you want me to ask him if you can be present for that?"

"Yes, please, I really would like to be present if it's possible. This waiting at home is enough to drive a person crazy." I really wished I could have been present for the entire trial and in one way I could understand the arguments from the defense counsel that it might prove sympathy from the jury if they saw me sitting in the courtroom. But, on the other hand, isn't that what Rossi was doing? He was sitting there in his suit and fresh haircut being passed off as an unfortunate, upstanding citizen, someone who is not really a bad, vicious person, rather a person who was insane at the time of this criminal act. Wasn't it the intent of the defense counsel to provoke sympathy for his client from the jury as well?

Wayne promised he would ask Mr. Garfield if I could be present for the closing day. I hung up the telephone, sat back in my chair, but was unable to return to my novel. My thoughts continued along the lines of my own rights—those which nobody else felt worthy of attention. I understood that he was the Defendant. He was the person who was innocent until proven guilty. He had the right to have his day in court and to be defended to the fullest extent that our laws allowed. But what about me? It was the State of Florida versus Rossi. I was just one of the witnesses who took the stand to substantiate the case for the prosecution. How cold, I thought, how totally unfeeling. I was the victim; if it weren't for me there would not have been any crime. They wouldn't be in that courtroom right now. I couldn't help feeling a little angry about the situation. I was not angry with the man who committed the crime but at the system which protected his rights over mine. Is this equality?

I was positive that we could get a conviction based on the physical evidence. Everything substantiated our case. Rossi admitted that he committed the crimes. However, the issue of insanity bothered me. Would the jury believe the testimony of the psychologist for the defendant? What if they did? How much time would he spend in a mental institution until he was found to be sane again?

This was not the first time he was arrested. I couldn't help thinking that he knew exactly what to do, he had proved this to me throughout that fateful night. He was cold and calculating: he was not naive or stupid. Now a psychologist takes the stand and states that this man needs help, that he is insane, and should be found not guilty.

I stood up and walked into the kitchen, I didn't know why. I pulled out a chair and sat down. "What was the worst that could happen? To be found not guilty by reason of insanity and put into a mental hospital." Those words, "not guilty," sounded frightening when said aloud. They were better just in my thoughts. I couldn't help recalling the horror stories of criminals who were put into a mental institution and then after only a few years were found to be no longer insane. Their crimes were repeated. I could not believe that this was actually happening to me. I hoped this would be taken into consideration by the jury when they were deciding Rossi's fate—and mine. I wondered, I just wondered, who would be responsible the next time if he were to be found not guilty by reason of insanity this time. How many times would the taxpayers have to pay to bring him to justice? Just the thought of him being released was terrifying. But a thought is not reality, and reality would not be known until Monday.

Later that evening, I was finishing my after-dinner duty of loading the dishwasher, when Kristin came running in to remind me of something that I had almost forgotten.

"Mommy, can I get dressed for Halloween? The boys are already putting on their funny makeup to look like monsters. You should see Shawn, his face is all green, and Marc has his face all white with black lines on it. Can I get ready now, too?"

"Do you know where your costume is?"

"Yes, I do."

"All right, then, you can go get dressed while I finish up here. If you need any help, just let me know." I heard Kristin go running through the living room and also heard her giggle as she passed by the bathroom door where her brothers were busy putting the finishing touches on their Halloween makeup. I heard her bedroom door shut. No sooner did her door close when I heard the familiar words, "Mommy, I need some help." I closed the door to the dishwasher and reached up to the cupboard that was left open, carefully closing that as well. I had to remind myself constantly that fast moves could be detrimental to my health. I walked through the kitchen where I heard the boys getting ready.

"Shawn, put a little more red around your mouth. It's not even enough. You have too much on the left side," I heard Marc say.

"How's that, any better?" Shawn asked.

"I can't get all my hair stuffed under this rubber cap. Do you think you can help, Shawn?"

Kristin spoke up again, "Mommy, are you coming?"

"I'm on my way, I'll be right there." I had been lingering outside the bathroom door listening to the boys' conversation, "Marc, I'll help you, I'll be right there as soon as I get finished with your sister."

I opened the door and walked into Kristin's room. Immediately she handed me the soft, fuzzy puppy costume. "Mommy, this is so cute. Did you really make this?"

"Yes, I made it for Shawn when he had a party at pre-school. He was just as old as you are right now." The touch of this costume brought back memories. This was one thing I did not have to have described to me. I remembered feverishly slaving over my machine, sewing every detail of the pattern for the puppy costume. It was only six years ago, something I had done in my past, that I would never again be able to do. I helped her with the suit and the zipper.

"Remember this, mom?"

"I sure do." She handed me the little hat that was made to match.

She walked over to the front of her bedroom mirror. "Oh, mommy, I look so cute, I wish you could see me." I just stood there facing where the voice was coming from.

"I wish I could, too, Kris, I really wish I could." I wondered if these feelings of hurt would ever stop. All the wishing and the hoping in the world would never bring my sight back. I put my arms around my daughter and gave her a hug. Even her wish was to restore my sight.

"Come on, Kris, I'll show you what I used to do for Shawn."

"What was that, mommy?"

"You can put some makeup on to make you look like a real puppy."

I told Marc that I would be there to help him in a second. I took Kristin by the hand and led her into my bathroom. I reached into my vanity drawer for the dark brown eyebrow pencil that I no longer needed. I took my left hand and placed it on her nose. Then I smeared some of the dark brown pencil on the tip of my finger and gently rubbed it across the tip of her tiny nose. I touched the side of her cheek, guiding the eyebrow pencil to make three streaks on each side of her nose for whiskers. I turned her around to look in the mirror, "Well, how does that look?"

"That looks cute, mommy. Now I look like a real puppy. Thanks mom."

"Marc, I'm on my way."

There, I thought to myself, mom wasn't helpless after all. I walked into the bathroom where the boys had been just standing, talking, looking into the mirror and admiring themselves while waiting for me to come in to help Marc. I put some powder on my hands and ran them through Marc's brown locks, "You just have too much hair." I pushed it all upwards and flattened it down. I took the rubber cap and gently slid it over the top of his head. Once it was in place, Marc and I tucked all the loose ends of his hair underneath the cap.

"Hey, mom, that looks pretty good."

I really felt pretty proud of myself.

"Mom, take a look at these." He took my hand and slowly guided it up to the side of his head. I ran my fingers along the outline of the large rubber pointed ear that covered my son's smaller one. I then continued to run my hand over the smooth bald cap and down the side of his other large rubber, pointed ear. A rather odd image flashed into my mind, that of my son with his face painted all white with highlights of black, a bald cap and two pointed rubber ears. I couldn't see it, but with his vivid description and my ability to "see" the way that I would now become accustomed to seeing, I was able to have a rather good image of what my son looked like. Shawn then described himself to me as well, the green face with the red mouth and the black eyes. They were all set and ready to go, my puppy and the two creatures from outer space.

Wayne took a look at the boys and couldn't contain his laughter. He handed them their plastic bags and followed them through the doorway.

My neighbor insisted on coming over to help me distribute the Halloween candy. She felt it would be much safer since I could not see who was at the door. Every time a child would yell, "Trick or Treat," or knock on the door, she was first to peek through the blinds, see who was there, and then very reluctantly open the door and distribute the candy.

When Wayne returned with the children, my neighbor left to go back to her home. "Sharon, if you need anything else, just let me know." I thanked her for her kindness, "You'd better rush home so that you can hand out some candy to your little trick or treaters, too."

"Oh, no! I'm going to go home and watch television in the back room. I never hand out candy to kids. In fact, I never open the door to anyone. My goodness, look what happened to you. You, of all people, should know you just cannot be too careful today." She did not give me a chance to reply to her statement. I felt a void where she had been standing. I heard her footsteps clamber across the street and fade into the distance. I remained at the open doorway until I heard her door slam shut. Paranoid, I thought. I wondered if she was always like that, or was she just using me as an excuse. I closed the front door but didn't have time to dwell on those thoughts.

"Mom, can you check our candy?" Shawn asked. Wayne and I took the three bags of Halloween goodies and carefully inspected each one, piece by piece. Was this also an act of paranoia? Definitely not, I reconfirmed. It was caution. There is definitely a difference. Paranoia can be disabling. It can stop a person from living life to its fullest. Caution, on the other hand, must be blended into each and every day. I knew that the key word was awareness, I had to make my children aware of the world around them, and its problems. I knew if they were aware, then they could take the precautions that could prevent a potentially dangerous situation. Inspecting the candy tonight was just one of those ways of preventing potential injury to my children. This caution had to be blended carefully into every day so the paranoia would not take over and fear would not consume every ounce of energy.

Halloween night was a much-needed distraction from the trial. But words like "insanity," "guilty" and "not guilty" were never far from my thoughts. I put the children to sleep giving them their hugs and kisses and even saying good-night the usual three or four times. I felt drained. I was absolutely exhausted from thinking, pacing, pondering and wondering. Even that little extra concentrating and preparing the children for Halloween contributed to my fatigue. "Wayne, I'm really tired. I'm going to go to sleep now. Is it all right with you?"

"I don't mind, I'm going to stay up and watch this movie. I don't know when I'll be to bed. Just go to sleep."

I walked into my bedroom, slipped off my jeans and slowly unbuttoned my blouse. I felt as though this day would never end. I walked over to the sink, brushed my teeth and washed my face. I reached for my hair brush and smoothed my hair softly on both sides. I checked my alarm to be sure it was set for the usual 7:00 a.m. I already knew it was set for that time, I had never any reason to change it, but for some reason, tonight, I found it necessary to recheck. I sat down on the edge of the bed and slowly took off my slippers. It was only Friday night, I had a whole weekend ahead of me. I laid down in bed again lost in thought. *"Oh, how I wish this whole thing were over; this waiting is absolute torture. I hate not knowing the outcome. I feel so helpless; there is nothing I can do. This whole thing is totally out of my control. The jury makes the decision: Those six people—the five women and one man. They are the ones who have control. The judge has it, too.*" I was worried that the jury would set this man free. And if he were found guilty, I was still worried that the judge would not regard the crime as serious and feel that a light sentence was sufficient.

"Why am I doing this to myself," I asked myself out loud. Why was I worrying about something over which I had no control? I had to be patient. I knew if I continued the way I was today, it was going to be the longest weekend of my life. I had to ask myself some very honest questions. How much more worrying did I want to give to the trial over which I had no control? My worrying was not going to have any bearing on the outcome of the verdict. I eased my thoughts by changing them to the things that I did control: What I was going to do this weekend. I turned over and pulled the covers over my shoulders. The breeze was cool blowing in the bedroom window. I thanked God for helping me make it through another day and I asked Him for the much needed strength to go on. I had done this ever since my childhood, and I had never forgotten. My prayers were answered as I drifted off to sleep.

I kept myself busy all weekend; I even went to the movies with the children. The children like going to the movies, and so do I. I tried getting in for half price by explaining to the cashier at the box office that since I received only half the benefits of the movies, I should be able to get in for half price. They never bought my explanations, though. I usually sat between Marc and Kristin and Wayne would sit next to Shawn. Once in a while the children would switch seats depending upon who felt like talking the most during the movie. Marc did such a marvelous job in explaining every detail on the screen that I visualized all the images as they were described. Kristin was very quick to correct him if she overheard his descriptions and disagreed. In the middle of the movie Kristin had to go to the ladies' room. And who, other than I, was there to take her? Quietly and discreetly, not to attract attention, I took hold of her shoulders and followed behind. Before Kristin opened the door to where we were supposed to be going, I double checked by asking her to read the letters that were posted on the door.

"Capital W-o-m-e-n, women, this is it, mom." She pushed through the double doors leading me inside. I waited patiently for Kristin and helped her wash her hands.

"Very good, Kris. Now let's get back to the movies."

Kristin reached for my hand and led me to the door. "Here's the door, mom," and she placed my hand on the handle. I felt a thick heavy chain with a padlock, "Kristin, this isn't the right door." Silence filled the room, and then a yell, "Oh, no, we're locked in here, there is no other door, we'll never get out of here!"

She started crying hysterically. I reached down and put my arms around her shoulders. "Wait just a minute, Kristin. Take me over to the sink. Now watch. Here's what we're going to do." I followed the wall closest to the sink, trailing it with my fingertips, following it all the way around the room. Once again I came to the door with the padlock, then continued on further. I found another door handle, "Look here," I said to my daughter.

"You found it, mom. I knew you would." Once again, she led me back to the double doors just as if nothing had ever happened. She led me back through the door to the theater and down the aisle where Wayne and the boys had been waiting. "I was ready to come looking for you two, I thought you got lost," Wayne whispered.

"We were stuck, daddy, but mommy saved us."

"What?"

I heard the surprise in Wayne's voice, "I'll explain later."

Mr. Garfield called on Saturday afternoon. He explained to me that the closing arguments would be heard Monday morning. He had checked with the public defender and the judge and there was no problem with my presence for the reading of the verdict. He suggested that I come down to the courthouse the first thing in the morning. There was no way of telling exactly how much time it would take for the jury's deliberation. I thanked him for his call and told him I would be there. Thoughts about the trial were only brief. I was determined not to let them get the better of today. I had already given them enough time yesterday. I continued with my household chores since cleaning now took extra care and concentration.

The rest of the weekend was taken up with grocery shopping and some window shopping at our local mall with the children and Wayne. Wayne reserved most of his comments, and shared only fleeting thoughts. I knew that since the day of the attack it was not easy for him. He would never be specific about what was on his mind or bothering him. He kept most of those feelings locked deep inside. At times the tension in the household was so thick you could cut it. Other times there was only silence. This weekend was quiet.

"Wayne, do you want to talk about it?"

"Talk about what?"

"Is something bothering you?"

"No, besides, I don't want to talk about it."

"Are you sure? It's usually best if you just get it out. I know I feel better if I talk about it."

"I told you, I don't want to talk about it."

The calm talking had taken on a loud, tense tone; I decided to drop the issue and leave well enough alone. It would take time; it was just going to take more time.

On Monday morning Wayne and I sat on the bench outside the courtroom waiting for Rick Garfield. The hallway in front of me was crowded with familiar and unfamiliar voices. The bailiff, Al, greeted us and then said he was glad I could finally come and attend the last day of the trial. I heard the familiar voice of Mr. Walsh mutter a hello as he passed by.

"Good morning, how are you holding up?" Rick asked moments later.

"As well as can be expected I guess."

I could detect a bit of nervousness in Mr. Garfield's voice, "First on the agenda is going to be the closing arguments. I had checked with the judge and I have some bad news for you. You will not be able to sit in the courtroom and listen to the closing arguments. We just can't take the chance of the jury seeing you present. The good news is, you can sit in the back room and listen through the door. Would you care to do that or do you want to wait out here in the hall?"

If they would not let me attend the trial, the best alternative I had was to listen to the closing arguments because they might summarize what had occurred. "Definitely, I would like to hear the arguments."

Wayne went inside the courtroom, and Rick led me to the back room where I was to be seated. He opened the door just a little and then left. I heard the familiar voice of Judge Kaplan passing by. The voice stopped directly in front of me.

"Good morning, Sharon, I hope you will be able to hear all right back here. After the closing arguments, I am going to go into one of the more boring portions of the trial. I have to instruct the jury. You can choose to listen or not. I will be instructing them about the law, and this is not usually very exciting. After I give the jury my instructions, they will retire to the jury room to deliberate. You can then be brought back into the courtroom for the reading of the verdict."

I thanked Judge Kaplan for his information. Then there was silence where his voice had been. All was quiet in the courtroom. I sat in a chair next to the door opened just a crack. I heard an elevator. The woman sitting behind the desk must have noticed the startled look on my face, "That must be Judge Kaplan. That noise you hear is a wheelchair lift that raises him up to his bench."

I did not realize that Judge Kaplan had been in a wheelchair. That would explain the missing footsteps when he left.

The noise in the courtroom had turned into silence. "All rise." I could hear everybody stand up. Judge Kaplan was ready to begin.

"Good morning," he said. "This is what we are going to do now: Both attorneys are going to make the closing statement to you. The statements that they make are not evidence. You have already heard all the evidence and each attorney will speak to you for the approximate same period of time.

"You can, if you like, accept the argument of one of the attorneys and reject the argument of the other one, or you can accept portions of each and reject portions of each. Whatever you decide, and if you are all ready to go now, we will have these closing arguments.

"Mr. Garfield, at this time if you are ready to proceed."

"Thank you, Your Honor," came Rick's voice. "If it please the Court, Mr. Walsh, Mr. Rossi, good morning, ladies and gentlemen.

"Although the judge has indicated to you that closing arguments of attorneys may help you, it's always been my feeling that I should not have to give one, because I think that the truth, especially in this case, should be self evident to you."

Rick Garfield proceeded to go over the charges that Rossi faced: Kidnapping, sexual battery, attempted murder—once with a gun, and then again with a knife.

"You may recall the medical testimony that she was stabbed in the chest, and that the stab wound went approximately four centimeters deep into her chest. I would submit to you that she was left for dead, just as Barbara Bay was in 1970, and that is one of the valid reasons you can consider the testimony of Barbara Bay."

Garfield's voice changed, became more urgent, as he began the second part of his closing arguments.

"Now," he said, "let's talk about this defense. First of all, there is no doubt that the defendant is not normal. Nobody, and I mean nobody who commits a kidnapping, a rape, and all these other things, is normal, but under our system such people are nevertheless punished unless they are legally insane.

"Let's look at some of the actions that the defendant committed during

this ordeal to see if he understood the quality of his acts, their consequences, and their wrongness.

"To begin with, let's look at the subterfuge or the trickery he used in
taking advantage of his victim. He used logic in determining that she,
Sharon Komlos, would come with him because she needed medical attention, just like he did with Barbara Bay.

"According to the testimony of Ms. Komlos, he said something to the
effect, 'Oh, my God, who could have done this?' Right there, what does
that tell? He certainly knew the consequences of the fact that she was in
grave medical danger—right from the beginning. The mere realization
on his part that she needed medical care tells you he knew the consequences of his actions right there.

"He told her that he had prior medical training in the service. Again,
a very indicative statement to make. It shows that he is trying to win
her confidence. He just took advantage of the situation and placed his
own needs and gratification of those needs above and beyond really
caring what happened to anybody else. Just him. That's all he was concerned about. This is an antisocial person. Knows the rules; knows the
consequences of violating those rules, but he has little or no regard for
the rules.

"What else? He conceals her in a car. Puts her down on the floor
between the rear seat and the back of the front seat. Why would he do
that? So nobody can see her. That's obvious.

"Continually tells her 'keep your head down,' if you recall her testimony.

"He had no trouble driving; certainly knew the consequences of driving
his car. He had no trouble obeying the traffic laws.

"You may recall she told him 'let's attract the attention of the police.'
That would get her an ambulance or get her help faster, and he didn't
want to do that for obvious reasons. He knew the police were the last
people he wanted there to intercept him. . .

"What did he do with the evidence in this case? You know that no
firearm was ever recovered. What did he do with that item?

"The police have collected some evidence for you. You know where
that evidence is. You can see that evidence, the things that were found
in his car in Miami.

"Ladies and gentlemen, look at that junk over there, if you want to.
If you could stomach it look at those bloody mattresses, sheets, pillows,
comforters, and everything else.

"Incidentally, I'd like to point something out to you. Here are two photographs that are in evidence. The first one shows the bed in the apartment when it was photographed at around ten o'clock or so that morning after this happened. You will notice that the bed is made. Somebody made this bed. Do you think Sharon Komlos made this bed?

"I'd like to show you something else." Rick Garfield held up the second photograph.

"See this mattress? It covered that pool of blood. You see? You may recall the testimony, and you can compare it to the original photograph. This had been turned upside down so that the bloody part was facing down, not up. This is the part you sleep on, but according to the detectives it had been turned over. Do you think Sharon Komlos did that? And why does somebody turn over a mattress but to conceal that? If you like you can see that exhibit in evidence—the bloody mattress cover.

"Finally, let's look at some of this expert testimony. I will just go in order.

"What I'm about to say is what I believe to be basically a summary of what Dr. Cohn told you from the witness stand. Mental status exam revealed: 'A rather normal functioning human being,' with intact memory. No delusions or hallucinations, and acceptable intelligence. Dr. Cohn gave you a diagnosis of sexual sadism, from the Diagnostic and Statistical Manual. Sexual Sadism is his diagnosis, an evaluation of neurosis—a relatively minor mental problem that everybody has. Not psychosis.

"As to Dr. Berntson—another one selected by Mr. Walsh—he did not see the transcripts of the defendant's lengthy statements to the police. In fact, he spent a total of three minutes—three minutes!—talking to the defendant about the very behavior you people are being asked to determine. Three minutes!

"Then Dr. Berntson administers a battery of neurological tests, some of which the defendant performs slowly; so of course he says he finds abnormality there. He told us that a normal person can do one of these tests in thirty-six seconds, but Mr. Rossi does it in thirty-nine seconds. If you want to be impressed by that, fine.

"Now we come to Dr. Eichert, a court-appointed psychiatric expert. Dr. Eichert, you may remember, has been superintendent of the state mental hospital in Maryland, the Crownsville State Hospital. He's been superintendent of the Florida State Hospital.

"Dr. Eichert found there was no history of prior adjudications of insanity. The defendant was mentally troubled, but not to the extent—not even sick enough—to be hospitalized against his will.

"Dr. Eichert questioned the defendant about the alleged offenses. And, like every other expert in the case, Dr. Eichert concluded that the defendant is sane enough to stand trial, and able to assist his counsel. Dr. Eichert said he knew the difference between right and wrong, and the nature and consequences of his actions at the time of the alleged crimes. He also testified that the defendant was not sufficiently mentally ill even to be put in a hospital against his will.

"So, that's about it. Is the defendant a mentally troubled person? Sure. Of course he is. People who do these things always are. But was the defendant insane as the law defines it for you at the time that he committed these crimes? Absolutely no way. No way whatsoever was he insane at the time of these offenses.

"It will be hollow words for me at this time to say to you people, 'let's do some justice in this case.' How are you going to do justice at this point? You can't...but the least I can ask you for is to satisfy your collective conscience as to the truth of this case. Let your verdict be a message to Thomas Edward Rossi."

Rick Garfield was done, and there was complete silence in the courtroom. Slowly, Bernie Walsh got to his feet.

"Ladies and gentlemen," he said, "right from the very beginning, from the first day I met you, from the first words out of my mouth, I told you that Tommy Rossi is the one who did it. I am not denying that. I was as open as I could be with you. He is the one who did it.

"The only issue I am here to talk about is one: Was that boy insane at the time of the crime? If Tommy, due to his mental defect, couldn't understand the nature and quality of his acts or the consequences of those acts; or if he couldn't distinguish right from wrong at the time of the crime, you must find him not guilty by reason of insanity.

"Now, there is an easy way out for anybody who sits on a jury like this. You can say to yourself, who cares?—let him get what he deserves! But, ladies and gentlemen, there are two ways of dealing with this. You have on this side the vicious criminal who knew what he was doing each and every time he did something—and he goes ahead and does it anyway and he gets what he deserves. He gets put where he belongs, and fine and dandy. I'm not saying anything is wrong with that. I'll be the last one to say that.

"Ladies and gentlemen, there is another person, the person who did not know what he was doing, or didn't know the consequences of his actions. And that person deserves proper treatment.

"Please, ladies and gentlemen, don't fall into that category, that rash, first gut reaction. It's easy to do—it's very easy to do.

"Before you make your decision, you must submit all the evidence to the balance of justice. This test of balance is the cornerstone of the entire criminal justice system. And it goes like this:

"If in your mind the facts are susceptible to two reasonable constructions, one indicating guilt, or sanity, the other indicating not guilty, insanity, and they are equal—you have that wavering—you must choose the one indicating not guilty, or not guilty by reason of insanity.

"Let's take those scales and do the test. What are you going to put on the one indicating guilt? Eichert...maybe. And what do you put on the other side? Dr. Cohn, who sees him three times over and over again. Dr. Berntson who sees him four times, has him report to his office and reviews all those reports.

"Your own common sense listens to the facts of the case from 1970 and says that only an insane person could have done it! You are not even dealing with equals. You have a scale that's been tipped over! Please, ladies and gentlemen, apply that foundation of criminal law with fortitude. Thank you."

There was only one more person who had to speak before the jury retired to reach their verdict: Judge Stanton Kaplan.

"Ladies and gentlemen," came the stern voice, "you have listened carefully to all of the evidence, and to the arguments of the attorneys. You alone as jurors sworn to try this case must pass on the issues of fact and your verdict must be based solely on the evidence or the lack of evidence and the law which I now am giving you."

The Judge reiterated all the charges against the defendant. He defined the terms kidnapping, sexual battery, and attempted murder, and he instructed the jury as the maximum and minimum penalties involved. Then, the Judge instructed the jury on the nature of criminal insanity.

"One of the defenses asserted in this case is that the defendant is not guilty by reason of insanity at the time of the alleged crimes. The law does not hold a person criminally accountable for his conduct while insane since an insane person is not capable of forming the intent essential to the commission of a crime.

"A person is sane and responsible for his crime if he has sufficient mental capacity when the crime is committed to understand what he is doing, and to understand that his act is wrong.

"If at the time of the alleged crime a defendant was by reason of mental infirmity, disease, or defect, unable to understand the nature and the quality of his act or its consequences, or if he did understand it, was incapable of distinguishing that which is right from that which is wrong, he was legally insane and should be found not guilty by reason of insanity.

"Insanity may be permanent, temporary, or may come and go. It is for you to determine the question of the sanity of the defendant at the time of the alleged commission of the crimes.

"Until the contrary is shown by evidence, the defendant is presumed to be sane. However, if the evidence tends to raise a reasonable doubt as to his sanity, the presumption of sanity is overcome.

"Now you know all the penalties, and you know what happens if the defendant is found not guilty by reason of insanity. I am now going to instruct you that you are to disregard the consequences of your verdict. You are impaneled and sworn only to find a verdict based upon the law and the evidence. Thus, you are to lay aside any personal feelings that you may have in favor of or against the State, or in favor of or against the defendant. It's only human to have personal feelings of sympathy in matters of this kind, but any such personal feeling or sympathy has no place in the consideration of your verdict.

"There is no time limitation upon you. Once you have all made up your minds don't sit back there. Just let us know, or if it takes you a very long time, that's all right, too. Whichever is your pleasure.

"With that, I will ask you to go back to the jury room now and deliberate your verdict."

It was three-thirty p.m. when the jury retired, and Rick Garfield came to visit me in the Judge's Chambers. He had admired Walsh's final speech, and he was very nervous that his words had swayed the jury to vote for acquittal.

Yet, for once, Rick was wrong. In only two hours, the jury returned with their verdict: Guilty on all counts. I was allowed in the courtroom for the sentencing, and I'll never forget the tone of Judge Kaplan's voice as he delivered the sentence.

"Mr. Rossi," he said, "as you heard, the jury found you guilty of kidnapping, sexual battery, and attempted murder in the second degree, two counts.

"We will start with Count One, Kidnapping. The Court at this time will sentence Mr. Rossi on the charge of kidnapping to be incarcerated with the Division of Corrections for a period of thirty-seven years. Mr. Rossi will not be eligible for parole on that particular offense without my permission. In that regard, and in regard to all of the charges, all the sentences which I'm now going to give, I will retain jurisdiction over one third of the sentence.

"My findings are I feel that the detention is justified. Mr. Rossi when he goes through these periods of explosion, exemplifies himself as a sadistic maniac. There is no woman on the face of this earth who is safe with him roaming the streets. He must be put away for as long a period of time as is possible."

So, Judge Kaplan gave Rossi maximum sentences, and the final total was 104 years in prison. The trial was over. I called my mom, told her the results, then heard her yell the news to the entire family. Then Rick Garfield and I went out for a drink, not so much in celebration as in sincere respect for the law. Whatever the flaws of our system of criminal justice, Thomas Rossi would be off the streets for a very long time—perhaps as long as I would be blind. Now, I said to myself, on to better things.

CHAPTER SEVEN

Christmas

Rossi may have received a long sentence, but he also got lifetime welfare at the expense of my neighbors and me. He had exchanged one victim for another, one jail for another in a nicer climate. Prison had clearly become a home to him. He would now receive health and medical care, food, clothing, recreation and entertainment, courtesy of my fellow taxpayers and me. His life would not be glorious, but nonetheless, he would be provided for.

My sentence was handed down not by a judge, but rather by Rossi. Mine, too, was for life—unsighted life. And I was going to have to find a way to provide for my children and me. Our family depended on two incomes, but we now had only Wayne's. It would put a strain on the household budget. Yes, I was free, I was alive, and I was now going to have to find a way to provide for my family in my new world of darkness.

I had dealt with all these feelings before, right after the incident occurred. The end of the trial marked the end of waiting. I knew that I could not lay plans for my future until it was over. It was now over, and I had to begin to take the steps that would carry me through the rest of my life.

I needed a new focus. I knew I could not return to my old job, but I was not excited about the job ideas the Blind Division had to offer. I had already dealt with the feelings of being blind for the rest of my life and had set my own path to rehabilitation. I wanted to find a way to go back to my old profession of insurance. If I could no longer be a Claims Adjuster, perhaps I could be a salesperson. I dug out the book from the back of my closet and felt the pages. It was the book from which I had taken the exams to earn my license as an Adjuster. I could take a new test to earn another license. I called the state capitol to find out if they made allowance for blind test takers. They did; I could give oral answers. I called Chuck and asked if he would help me. He said that he would. I told Wayne about the project, but he was not enthusiastic.

About all he could squeeze out was a very reluctant, "That's nice." If it had been up to Wayne, I suspect that I would not have had a career, but he could not earn enough by his own efforts to feed and house and transport us.

Day-to-day living with Wayne was increasingly difficult. I thought this situation would ease a little after the trial, but I was wrong. Talking was very difficult; he would begin shouting instead. I had a feeling that somehow he felt violated, that his life had been ruined at the hands of this man. I felt that the bitterness and anger were directed towards me. I hoped that since talking only provoked arguments that not talking would produce more thought and concentration. I kept hoping that somehow he would be able to think things through and overcome what had happened. I thought maybe time would heal some of the wounds. I had lost hope that Wayne would be a major source of support in my efforts to develop a full life for myself.

I had no hope in getting that support from the social welfare agencies. They simply did not have my welfare in mind. I had never completely lost contact with the Division of Blind Services, and in late November I was paid a visit by a supervisor of the Division. She came because of unfinished paperwork—their need, not mine. The sporadic visits I had received from them since June were anything but useful to me.

The supervisor who appeared in November was a tall woman, and her voice came from a point far above my head. I invited her in and she sat down, and started to talk. She congratulated me on the outcome of the trial and made a few suggestions about the punishment the criminal should receive. Her suggestions were very creative. The conversation then took a more serious note, "I understand that you don't want to learn Braille." I told her that I felt Braille was not for me. I explained my position that Braille was not the only way for a person to be mainstreamed into the sighted world. She expressed her opinions and her reasons. She said it had been tried and true for many years, and it was the only way, and I should reconsider. She stated that she was going to order some mechanical aids for me. She would include a Brailler machine that could type in Braille. I asked her reasoning behind ordering such an expensive piece of equipment since I did not know Braille and I had no intention of learning it. She told me regardless of what I felt she was going to order it. She also became more adamant than the previous woman about the fourteen-week trip to Daytona. I asked her about provisions for my three children, and she advised that I would have to make all the necessary arrangements, that they would not provide any type of care in my absence. She stated that in Daytona they would teach me how to cross a four-lane highway by myself, proper use of the cane and how it would be my protection. They would also teach me tips on inside mobility, care and personal grooming, independent living skills in the kitchen, and how to walk up and down steps. I wanted to ask what she thought I had been doing for the past six months, but I didn't. I had already done everything she had listed, except for crossing the four-lane highway by myself, and I felt there was no need to prove to someone that I could tap my way across a four-lane highway when I would not have done this in my days of 20/20 vision. I told her I had already done everything she said that they would teach me. She then said that I could share some of my own personal tips with other people who were unsighted. I told her, and was very adamant, that it was more necessary for me to stay at home with my children than spend fourteen weeks away from home. I told her I would not go. She filled out the paperwork and would not take no for an answer. She told me that there were some other forms for me to sign, those for the request for the equipment. Along with the list of the Brailler was included a talking calculator and some mobility aids. I felt those would be of some use so I signed the document. She told me she would show me how to sign the paper the way that the blind did, and when I scribbled down my signature, she seemed a bit surprised. She told me that was just one more thing I would have to learn: How to write the way that the blind did. I just let her comment pass. I was satisfied with my signature.

After the paperwork was completed, the woman left. I had the feeling I was going to go down in their records as being incorrigible. But their method of dealing with the newly blind defied all of my logical reasoning. I couldn't understand why they were so adamant upon rehabilitating someone according to how they felt she should be rehabilitated. Never once did they take into consideration my lifestyle prior to losing my sight. Never once did they ask me what I wanted or what I needed. The things I really wanted to learn I knew that they could not teach. How could I drive my car and how could I watch my children grow? Those were the two things that I missed the most, and they couldn't teach me that in Daytona.

I continued to add to my list of accomplishments within the household. I could cook, bake, wash clothes, sew, iron, make the beds, dust and vacuum. I tried a method of organizing my kitchen cupboards but anyone who has three children knows that any method of organization does not last very long. I finally relented to a system of disorganized organization.

It worked best for me. I even became rather good at putting groceries away. Once in a while Wayne or the children found things that were misplaced, but who cared if a box of Kleenex was in the freezer? The children just thought I was doing something new. I became adamant with my safety precautions around the home and rules governing certain items in the bathroom. I stressed to my family that tubes of ointment were not to be left on the bathroom counters next to the toothpaste. By experimenting around the house I found that I was capable of doing more things than I first thought. But Wayne and the children drew the line when I started matching socks. In self-defense they offered to do it themselves.

I did not just limit my duties to those around the house. I enjoyed getting out and shopping, even though window shopping was out. I still attended school functions, PTA meetings and even a field trip with Shawn's class. I baked cookies for boy scout functions and more cookies for the classrooms. I hemmed pants and sewed on patches and even went to the movies, even though I didn't get in for half price. I still enjoyed going out with Wayne in the evenings. Wayne and I went out on many occasions, and I was still good at fast dancing, if my partner promised not to leave. I enjoyed my life. My actions did not always go unnoticed, and there were those who still offered their opinions. I was getting good at ignoring the most insensitive comments and taking the others with a grain of salt. The insensitivities were easy to write off. They were usually by passersby or onlookers. They were people I did not know or who did not know me. Again I had to face the reality that those people would always be there and that I was going to be the one who was going to have to make the adjustments.

There were still some bad moments of bitter regret at my loss. Christmas was a time that evoked those moments, because it always was a special time for me. It meant family, love, peace and—now that my childhood years were long gone—reminiscing about those same holiday feelings that bring out the child in all of us. It meant another trip to Ohio. Being in my parents' house rekindled those old memories. Those vivid sights were locked into my memory, the Christmas tree in front of the window where it had always been, the Christmas cards hung around the archway between the living room and the kitchen. And my mother's small wooden nativity set placed just so under the Christmas tree. The scent of pine from the tree and the bayberry from the scented candles were part of the seasonal aromas. There was the familiar smell of baking that filled my mother's kitchen. One thing was for sure, I didn't have to see Christmas to feel it; its aura was ever-present and its memories locked deep in the heart and soul.

"Mommy, you should see this ornament, it's shiny and blue and on the front there's Bambi."

Slowly I walked over to the Christmas tree where Kristin was standing. She had found the ornaments that were my favorites when I was her age. "Kris, if you look around a little further, you'll find Snow White, and Thumper, too."

Kristin continued to guide my hand over the old ornaments as well as some of the new. There were white doves and little angels. She described the colors so vividly I could imagine their appearance exactly.

"Grandma, can I have a candy cane?" Kristin asked.

"Go ahead, Kristin, and get one for your brothers, too," the boys came running quickly when they heard that.

Wayne took our suitcases upstairs, and brought down the gifts to place under the Christmas tree.

"Well, kids, it's time to get ready for bed. We all have a busy day tomorrow. It's Christmas Eve and you know what that means," I said to the children with a little excitement in my own voice.

The boys knew what it meant and stood by silently while Kristin screamed it out loud, "We get to open our presents tomorrow night!"

My mother helped get the children ready for bed. They marched upstairs, off to bed without any argument, as would be expected of good children, especially the night before Christmas Eve.

Wayne sat in the living room watching television and my mother and I adjourned to the kitchen for a cup of tea. "Well, how's everything in Florida? I bet you miss the snow, don't you."

"To be honest with you, mom, I do miss the light, fluffy snow that falls so gently on Christmas Eve, but what you're having right now, I don't miss at all."

"How is Chuck?"

"He's doing just fine. Right now he's making the rounds to all the Christmas parties in the area. We even went to one of them with him. Chuck had a wonderful suggestion, mom. Chuck, Wayne, the children and I all went up to see the Christmas tree in Lantana. Chuck has been trying to get me there ever since the day I moved down, but it was not until now that we really had the time. From what I was told, mom, it's really a magnificent sight. It's the largest Christmas tree in the area. It's 121 feet tall with ornaments the size of basketballs and they use miles of garland. We went up there just in time to see the lighting of the tree."

I paused for a moment remembering the feelings that I had, "The kids said it was really a sight, mom. They said it was just beautiful. You could hear the 'oohs' and the 'aahs' from the crowd when the switch was thrown to turn on the lights. Mom, I strained to see those lights, I really tried. I couldn't help it, I started to cry. I was just glad it was dark outside so that Shawn, Marc and Kristin couldn't see my crying. Chuck was too busy joining in the excitement with the children, talking about how beautiful the sights were, that nobody even noticed me standing there all alone behind them all, crying. I guess it's something I'm just going to have to learn how to live with, right?"

I ended my sentence with a question, seeking some sort of a confirmation from my mother, as if I had a choice. I knew there were no choices. I could either live with it and get on with my life or let it destroy me. This was not the first time I wished I could see something and knew that I couldn't. I knew it wouldn't be the last.

"You are entitled to cry, you know."

I felt the warmth and consolation in my mother's voice and knew that she was right. It was all right to cry. It was a human emotion. If I felt it, I could do it.

We briefly discussed the trial. My mother still had a lot of questions to which we had no answers. Why did he do it in the first place? Why didn't he receive the death penalty?

I explained to my mother that it is not always easy to understand and live by the guidelines laid down by our criminal justice system. "Mom, it was a learning experience for me. Never before did I even have to appear in court, never before was I ever the victim of anything. When you go through it firsthand, you begin to understand why we call it the criminal justice system. The criminal receives all the justice."

My mother continued with her questions, "Why is it like that? What can we do to protect ourselves against people like this? Who is really to blame? I don't know, Sharon, the whole situation seems hopeless. All the time, you read in the newspapers about things like this happening, but you never ever think that it's ever going to happen to your family. It all seems so unfair. Where will it stop?"

All of the conversation about violence, crime, and our criminal justice system just died with my mother's last remark. It was Christmas time, and I wanted all of the attention to be reserved for the love and holiday spirit to which I had always been accustomed. "We'd better get to sleep. With the excitement of tomorrow, the children will be up at the crack of dawn, and you know they're going to be a handful."

My mother walked over and shut off the television. I walked over to the chair where Wayne had been sitting. Softly I called his name, and when I received no response, I realized he had fallen asleep. I shook him gently and woke him to go upstairs to bed.

Memories of the past can be a blessing. I was fortunate, I had those sights to recall. The bright colors of Christmas, the tree, the stockings, the snow outside, the excitement on the faces of my mother and father when they watched us open our Christmas presents. Those were the Christmases of my youth, those in my sighted days. I even had the opportunity to share some of those Christmases with my children. Those days in which I could see them. Now it was going to be different. This was my first unsighted Christmas, the first one when I could not store those sights a parent treasures for a lifetime. Just like photographs that freeze time on paper, my memories were frozen. All in my family were locked in physical state of how they looked when I last saw them; that was how I would remember them forever.

Shawn, Marc and Kristin were all naturally very excited. All three of them were very verbal in expressing themselves. The boys were older and remembered Christmas at my mother's house. But for Kristin, it was different. She was too young to recall the last time she was at my parents' home. She did not remember all the sights, sounds and smells that were associated with a Christmas in the household where I grew up. She sat on my lap unwrapping her presents, describing each one so vividly that I could paint my own visual image. Her Barbie doll, the color of the dress, the earrings, the ring. I could feel her excitement and imagine the look on her face. All of a sudden, it was no longer necessary to see her. The boys were equally vocal. It seemed as though my loss of sight gave them a new license to become more vocal, more excited, and more descriptive. They had to describe things so I could visualize them. They let me feel, and experience their Star War toys in order to get a good sense of what they were. I remembered seeing the movies, and now I could relate what each character looked like by following the forms of the molded plastic figures. I could understand more fully their method of travel by touching each piece of aircraft. I knew I had a lot to learn, and every new experience was the best teacher. My children took an active part in my learning. I didn't mind being taught by my own children; they have a lot to offer, and there is nothing wrong with seeing life through the eyes of a child. My first unsighted Christmas was happy. It was filled with love.

A New Career Opportunity

The love and joy of a family Christmas gave me back a lot of the strength that had been sapped by my ordeal, my adjustment to blindness, and Rossi's trial. I began to enjoy trips to the stores to shop. I was totally accepted by my neighbors and by my children, but I was rather naive in thinking that society, the people outside my little world, would accept me as I was. Since people tripped over my cane when I used it shopping in the malls, I stopped using it completely. I never thought how it would look if a woman was holding onto another woman's arm, nor did I really care. There were always some obstacles no matter where I went; I would either brush up against, run into, or trip over something along the way. I could not see the awkward glances or the unusual stares from the people around us, but occasionally I could pick up on a few of the comments. "Look, Helen, she must be loaded, and it's only mid-afternoon," or, "Why don't you watch where you're going?" which was the most common. I became more aware of how discourteous and unthoughtful people are sometimes. I would get bumped, shoved, and run into by people in a hurry to get from one place to another. I am blind, but in their own way they have to be blind too because they can not see another human being occupying the space in front of them. I became very good at dodging voices for my own safety. I also found that people were very curious. "Oh, my poor dear, how did you lose your sight, diabetes?" I heard a woman ask as we were both standing in front of the meat case in a butcher shop. I answered, "No, it was a gun." I heard her shriek and shuffle off to the other side of the counter. I figured, if she wanted to know, I'd tell her. Some people were courteous, others were not. Some treated me as a helpless poor soul, others; like I had a contagious disease from which they must keep their distance. When I spoke with some people, their reply would come out loud, clear and crisp. They would enunciate and shout. I would politely tell them that they had the wrong disability. My hearing was fine, it was my sight that I had lost. One of Shawn's friends asked me if I knew sign language. Again I replied, "Wrong disability." I found that getting shot was just the beginning. I found that my loss of sight gave me entry into a world of submerged attitudes. It was a world with which I was totally unfamiliar. I had never been around anyone who was blind, and I really didn't know how I would ever treat them. Now I was blind myself. I didn't know what was expected of me. I didn't know the rules or how to play the game. I only knew how to be me.

Virtually every person I met was curious. Directly or indirectly the topic of conversation would turn to how I lost my sight. When I would tell the unbelievable story of the shooting, usually the reaction was predictable. "Oh, my dear, I'm terribly sorry. You seem to have coped so well. You have to keep a positive attitude, you know. I had an uncle once who was blind, I did not really know him but those who did said he was a fabulous man and could do anything." I heard personal stories repeatedly about someone who was blind and could do the most fabulous things. I heard stories of blind runners and golfers, and mountain climbers. I never did any of these things when I could see, and blindness didn't increase my interest in them. I had my own list of priorities, my own list of things that I wanted to continue to do.

I never slipped into that deep, dark depression that many people asked about. They seemed so concerned with its length and severity. "Was I worried about sliding back into it?" It seemed that everyone believed that depression is the normal course of action after facing any type of tragedy. Some even felt it was necessary. I had an attorney who was handling some personal matters for me. He felt that we would be helped if I underwent psychological therapy. "I want you to see a friend of mine. He's a psychologist who will be able to document that within one year from the loss of your sight and the rape you will go through a very severe state of depression. We will need this to substantiate our case, and from what I understand, it is the normal course of events. I just want to document that it will occur." I very quickly objected.

"How does he know?" I asked my attorney.

His reply was, "It's normal."

I still objected. I questioned who lays down the definitions of "normal." Since everyone is an individual with his or her own way of thinking, of handling stress, of dealing with tragedy, and of meeting trials and tribulations, I really couldn't see one "normal" for everyone to follow. Was I normal? I thought I was. I knew that I was the only person who had control over the path that my life was going to take, only I could tell how I was feeling at any given moment, and only I could tell what I was going to do today and tomorrow. As for the future, did anyone really know what the future held? For the present, I was determined to control my life as much as possible and leave depressions to the victims.

Opinions of others can be very difficult to handle when they are expressed whether or not you want to hear them. They can make you question yourself when you shouldn't be questioning yourself at all. They can make you doubt your own capabilities and strengths. I figured that since I would hear other people's opinions whether I wanted to or not, I would ignore them and take responsibility for myself. The only way to avoid those unwanted opinions was to stay at home and hide. I had been at home for months and I knew that that was not the place for me. I knew a career would take me out into the public. I would be exposed to everyone, to those who were narrow-minded and even closed-minded, to those who would accept me and to those who would reject me. I would have to be prepared for it all. I would have to be flexible to handle any situation. Going out and shopping during the day, lunches in the afternoon, movies with the children, and even dancing at night were preparing me to take part in the working world once again. My training was almost complete. My self-confidence was high.

I hoped that a more independent me would be exactly what Wayne would want. After all, we needed more money than he was able to earn. But nothing I did helped. The tension grew within the household. He did not want to hear anything about my new career choices. He didn't want to hear what I did during the day. He only complained about his daily chores and about how rough he had it. If I was happy and excited, he was depressed and angry; if I wanted to go out, he wanted to stay in; if he wanted to go out, he did not want to go with me. All lines of communication had broken down. Every discussion became an argument. From the very beginning of my blindness, Wayne would occasionally leave the sharp knives in the dishwasher with the point up or would move the furniture. I had frequently been injured by those actions. It was something I could not overlook and could not control. Separation was inevitable.

Just when we had reached this point, one night, I was at a party that included Wayne and Chuck. A woman joined us whose husband played in the band. There was some good-natured discussion that a book would be a good idea. She said that she knew just the right person for me to talk with and promised to give him my name and telephone number. I forgot the episode because people frequently offered help without delivering.

The following Tuesday morning, I got a telephone call.

The deep male voice on the other asked, "Is this Sharon? My name is Wayne Dyer. A friend of ours told me to give you a call."

I was rather stunned to hear his voice, "Yes, well, hello," I really didn't know what to say.

He picked up the conversation, "She said you're quite a woman. I read about you in the newspapers also. I'd like to get together some day so that we could meet in person. Maybe I could help you. She said something about writing a book?"

"It was just a passing thought. I was provoked by some friends, but didn't take it seriously."

"I would like to meet you anyway; do you ever get down to the Fort Lauderdale area?"

"Well, I don't drive, even though I still have my driver's license. I don't have a car; I think my husband sold it because he knew I would be tempted to try it again." I heard him laugh in the background, "But seriously, yes, occasionally a friend will drive me down to Fort Lauderdale."

Wayne Dyer gave me his telephone number and address and told me to call before coming down. "I'll look forward to meeting you in person then."

"Thank you for calling, Wayne."

My first thoughts turned to that young woman that I had met earlier in the week. "She was the first person who ever kept a promise like that," I said to myself. Now I had to work on my ride.

The following Sunday afternoon, my brother was in town for Spring Break, "Sharon, would you like to come down and visit? By the way, do you have a few dollars I could borrow?" I knew he had an ulterior motive for inviting me down to Fort Lauderdale. My thoughts then turned to Dr. Dyer.

"Rick, let me call you right back. I'll see if I can get a ride." I called a friend to ask her what she was doing this delightful Sunday afternoon. Mary thought it would be a great idea and thought after we met with Rick we could even pack a picnic lunch and spend some time on the beach. "It will be a nice outing. We haven't seen each other in a while, and it would be good for the both of us."

"Mary, there's one more thing, there's a Dr. Dyer..." On the way down to the hotel where my brother had been staying, I explained to Mary the telephone conversation with Dr. Dyer. I told her that he was expecting us and handed her the piece of paper on which I had written his oceanfront address.

"Who wrote this?" she asked.

"I did."

"It looks like it."

"Don't critique my handwriting, just drive."

My brother, Rick, met us in the outer lobby of the hotel. I introduced him to my friend, Mary, and we sat and talked for a while. "How are the kids?" Rick asked.

"They're just fine; they're home right now with Wayne. Why don't you stop up and see them later in the week?"

"I will, I have some laundry to wash as well."

I reached in my pocket and gave Rick the ten dollars he had requested. I gave him a hug and left him with some sisterly advice, to be careful during his stay.

"You sound just like mom."

"Don't forget, I'm a mother, too."

Mary helped me to the car, and we went to see Dr. Dyer.

"Hi, there, come on in. Where would you like to sit? Would this be all right?"

Mary guided me over to the sofa in the middle of the living room. I was unfamiliar with this man, not knowing exactly who he was or what he did. Very quickly I was enlightened. Wayne asked me if I had ever considered public speaking as a career choice. I confessed that it never crossed my mind. He told me that he had two ideas. He had an idea for a magazine article. He wrote articles for a national publication, and he would like to do one about me. The second was, that he would arrange my first talk in front of a woman's organization in Fort Lauderdale.

"But what would I say, what would I talk about?"

He gave me some helpful hints, "Talk about yourself, about your past, talk about what brought you to Florida. Talk about that incident, the night of May 23rd. And lastly, talk about yourself now, how you have, and how you haven't changed." He made it sound so easy.

Wayne kept his promises on both counts. Inteviews began immediately for an article done for *Family Circle*, and early the following week, that same young woman who introduced me to Wayne Dyer made the necessary arrangements for a talk in front of one of the local women's organizations. The date was set for the first week in April. All I had to do was gather my thoughts and formulate them into a twenty-minute presentation. I remember the words of my college professor in Business Speech 101. "Use notes, always use notes. Never give anything longer than a two minute impromptu speech without your note cards." I remembered some of the other helpful hints, such as maintaining eye contact with your audience, and using visual aids such as flip charts and slides. He stressed that speaking was an art, that it was important to build a rapport with your audience from the start, and that it was important to read your audience. He taught us that their facial expressions and their body language were good indications of a presentation's reception. These tips were now useless to me. I was going to have to find my own way.

I remembered my first presentation in speech class: The sweaty palms, the shaky voice, and the loss of concentration. I guess these were characteristic of stage fright. I remembered my earlier days of baton twirling competition. Large crowds never bothered me then. Once into the routines, all of their faces disappeared anyhow. I guessed I would be able to compare a presentation to a performance. I could not use notes; therefore, preparation was of the utmost importance. I could not use flip charts or visual aids; therefore, my gestures would have to be just right. I could not read the faces or the body language of my audience; I would just have to listen very carefully for some sort of response. I would not be able to see my audience, but that was not all bad. I could always imagine a small group whether twenty or two hundred people were present. The more I thought about this new challenge, the more exciting it became.

I told my husband about the up-coming engagement. I really wanted him to be a part of it. I asked him for suggestions, about what he felt would be important to relate to my audience. I could not understand his lack of enthusiasm. "Don't think I'm going to drive you to these things. That's ridiculous." He stomped out of the room leaving me sitting at the kitchen table all alone, trying to figure out what happened. I couldn't help feeling angry. Why wasn't he supportive? Why was it every time I had an idea, it was worthless to him? It seemed as though I never did anything right. Where was that strong male figure, the one I read about in novels and watched in the made-for-television movies? Where was that strong supportive figure, that constant voice of reassurance, who told his wife when she was faced with a seemingly insurmountable tragedy, "Don't worry, dear, we'll make it through together." What happened to those words, "In sickness and in health and for better or for worse." It became apparent that I was not going to have that cheering section. I was not going to have that encouragement from the sidelines that every woman needs. I remember telling him back in the hospital, when I was lying on the gurney in the emergency room, that he shouldn't worry, that I was going to be just fine, that everything was going to be all right. I told him I was going to be fine, but he never told me that he would be. I wondered why he couldn't be supportive. I wondered where he thought he was drifting to.

I sat in the kitchen all alone, I heard footsteps enter, "Mom, you're sitting here with the lights out," said Shawn.

"I guess I just forgot to turn them on."

"You look upset about something, what's wrong." I was never very good at hiding my feelings.

"Nothing's wrong, I'm just thinking." I told Shawn about the presentation I was going to be giving next week. At least he thought it was a terrific idea.

"Today in school our teacher asked us to write about a person we admired. You know who I picked?"

"Who?"

"I picked you, mom. And then she wanted to know why we chose the person we did. And then she made us tell what lesson we learned from that person. Do you know what I told her?"

"No, what did you tell her?"

"Here, mom, let me read it to you. 'I think my mom is terrific. She really has a lot of courage. She was shot by a man and now she is blind, but don't feel sorry for her, because she does not feel sorry for herself. I think she is very brave and strong. The lesson I learned from my mother is that life isn't easy. I love her very much. And I am happy that she is still my mom.' "

The tears started to flow quick and fresh, and I wrapped my arms around my son.

"Do you like it, mom, is it all right?"

I wiped away my tears, "It was absolutely beautiful, Shawn. I really love it. . . Don't you think it's getting a little late?"

"I know, mom, it's time for bed. I already brushed my teeth, so did Kristin and Marc. Good night, I'll see you in the morning."

I heard the footsteps start to walk away. "Shawn, can I keep that?"

"Sure, mom." I heard his footsteps return, and he placed the sheet of paper in my hands. I reached out and gave him another hug. "By the way, I love you, too." He said good night again and I heard his footsteps leave.

He was so grown up, so wise, and he was only ten. They all had a crash course in reality. I could only hope and pray that they would not harbor anger and bitterness that could destroy the rest of their lives. Shawn's paragraph reassured me. I inclined my head toward the piece of paper I was holding in my hand. Gently I rubbed my fingertips over it, not knowing if I was touching the words which he had written or not. It then occurred to me. I had my own little support system, I had my cheering section. I had Shawn, I had Marc, and I had Kristin. Together, we were going to make it.

On the day of my first speech, I was not nervous—I was absolutely terrified. Mary took an extended lunch hour so she could drive me to the luncheon presentation hosted by an organization of executive women in the Fort Lauderdale area. Once a month they met to share information and hear presentations of useful information on women's issues. Would they really be interested in me? Many sleepless nights and countless hours of preparation went into this first presentation.

"What, no notes?" Mary asked.

"No, I thought I'd just wing it."

How could I possibly wing it for twenty minutes? Since I was the topic, I knew the information cold. I worried that if I got off track I had nothing to get me back. I knew it was going to take a lot of concentration. How could I come across at ease, and still keep my concentration? I had the feeling I was about to find out.

Mary parked in the handicapped spot in the hotel parking lot. She guided me inside, first checking in the lobby to see where the woman's organization was meeting. We were met there by a young woman waiting for us. "You must be Sharon, just follow me."

While walking down the hall, I went over the presentation in my mind trying to be sure I would not forget anything. The woman introduced us to the women around the table. Mary and I sat down to a deluge of questions.

"What company are you with?" I told them about my previous career. At the present time I was "between jobs." Surprisingly, none of the women inquired about my loss of sight.

"Would you like anything from the bar ma'am?" I continued thinking about my talk. "Ma'am, would you like anything from the bar?" Mary kicked me under the table.

"She's talking to you." I turned my head toward the voice of the young lady who had been trying to get my attention at the end of the table.

"I'm sorry, yes, please. I would like a glass of white wine."

Maybe this whole thing wasn't such a good idea. Maybe, just maybe

Wayne Dyer was wrong in setting this whole thing up. Why would they want to hear me in the first place? What did I have to offer these successful, professional women? We would soon find out.

The president of the organization stood behind the lectern with microphone in hand and had each one of the women stand up, identify herself, and give some professional background. The president then took the microphone and started the business meeting.

"I understand from our program chairman that we have a rather interesting speaker this afternoon. I'm not going to delay any longer, but I am going to turn the honors over to her to introduce your guest speaker for this afternoon."

Silence filled the room. The woman sitting next to me stood up and walked over to the microphone. Everyone was listening intensely to what she had to say.

"Your guest speaker for this afternoon is a most remarkable woman. She has undergone a tragedy in her life, but has survived the ordeal and is here to tell you about it. I have introduced her to my friend, Dr. Wayne Dyer, who has also found her remarkable. He is currently writing a story about her for a national magazine which will be published in early Fall. It is without further hesitation that I introduce to you, your speaker for this afternoon, Sharon Komlos."

A loud burst of applause filled the room. I sat in my chair in a state of shock. Mary kicked me under the table and at the same time reached for my arm jolting me out of my state of fright. She guided me up to the lectern and placed the microphone in my hand. I was on. My palms were sweating, my knees were shaking. Those horrible memories of Speech 101 flashed in my mind. *My God, where do I start? I thought I knew this.* I started by thanking the program chairman for inviting me to share my story with her organization.

"I was a career woman, and I'm the mother of three children. I am not a native Floridian. I moved to Florida in January of 1979. Life had been very good to me. I had my career, my three children, and we had just purchased a new home. It was May 23, 1980 when an event occurred that changed my life."

I told them about the incident that had taken my sight, carefully touching only on the more important aspects of that night of terror. I did not go into the gory details because my intent was not to frighten my audience, rather to inspire and motivate them. I described the recuperative process in the hospital, and how I decided right then and there that I was not going to waste time in getting started. I told them little about the children, and what I felt they had learned. I talked about life now, how it was changed, not destroyed by this act of violence. I couldn't think of anything else to tell them. I closed by thanking them for inviting me. Instantly, the room was filled with applause. They were actually clapping for me. Then I heard the noise level in the room rise. I heard the noise of the chairs bumping the tables. The applause continued. The meeting planner came over to me and took the microphone from my hand. She whispered in my ear, "They're giving you a standing ovation." The meeting planner then asked if the audience had any questions. Once again she turned the microphone over to me. Again silence filled the room, "There is only one thing that I ask of you," I told the women, "I ask that you don't raise your hand to be recognized, it won't do a thing for me." Laughter filled the room and I could sense someone was sitting there with her hand raised.

"What happened to the man who shot you?" Much to my chagrin, I had totally forgotten about Rossi and that is exactly how I began answering the question. I explained to the woman that he stood trial and was sentenced in early November. I told them about Judge Kaplan maintaining jurisdiction over one-third of the sentence, and that he would not be eligible for a parole hearing until Judge Kaplan gave his approval.

The questions continued, "How long did it take you to pull yourself out of the state of depression?" I answered this question by explaining my own rehabilitation process while in the hospital. I also quipped that I lived in the State of Florida, not in the state of depression. They approved of my humor. It was looked upon as in good taste rather than flip or inappropriate. "I don't really detect any anger in your voice. If this would have happened to me, I would want some sort of revenge against this man. Do you?"

I was finding out that I had to learn how to think quickly on my feet, "I feel that my attacker is being punished adequately for his crime. The State took care of that. As for the anger, it is a natural human emotion, but can be detrimental to one's well-being. It probably was there at one point, although I really don't recall for how long. I guess I just look at things a little differently. I felt that if I give in to anger or hatred, these two negative emotions that take a lot of time and energy, I would be giving this man more of my life. He has already taken enough. He has taken ten hours of my life along with my eyesight, and I am not about to give him anymore. I can talk about him openly and freely but I don't live in the past. I really can't help feeling a little pity for him. He is not now nor has he ever probably been a happy person. I have three lovely children and my life, I have happiness and their love. Isn't that what's important in life?"

"We have time for just one more question," the program chairman stated. "Yes, the lady way in the back."

"Sharon are you planning on writing a book? Let me just state that I really hope you are because I would like to read your story over and over again. So many times we get depressed in our lives and I feel that you could be doing all of mankind a service by putting your philosophies down in writing."

I laughed a little at the question. "At one point, yes, it was a passing thought. Now that you bring it up, I may give it more thought. Thank you for inquiring and for the words of encouragement."

Once again applause filled the room. I handed the microphone to the program chairman. I searched in the darkness for Mary's voice. "Sharon, I just wanted to tell you what a magnificent person I think you are. You don't realize how much you've helped me personally. Thanks again." The woman's hand touched mine then was removed.

Another voice came out of the darkness, "Sharon, I hope I didn't distract you too much when I left the room. I had to leave to call my office and tell my boss that I was going to be late. I hope I really didn't miss too much. I usually leave the meeting early so that I can get back to work, but this time I didn't want to miss one minute of your presentation. I thought it was absolutely fantastic. Keep on going. Thank you so much."

Finally Mary made it to the front of the crowd. "There are still quite a few who would like to talk with you."

"I was sexually assaulted about three years ago. I wish I could have heard you back then."

I could not see their faces. Their voices were all different. Each had another story to tell. It was such a wonderful feeling to be able to help other women. I had never felt this joy before. Could Wayne Dyer have been right? Could a speaking circuit really be a profession? I was attracted to the prospect.

By mid-April, only one week after my first presentation, I had three more talks scheduled. There were two to women's organizations for luncheon meetings, and one to a Methodist church in Fort Lauderdale. That first presentation opened a whole new world for me. I found myself beginning to analyze and question myself more deeply on the issues that were brought up during the question and answer periods. Why didn't I go through a state of depression? Why did I do things so quickly? Why wasn't there that expected long period of rehabilitation? I started listening more carefully to other speakers. I noticed they used quotes and catchy phrases. They used acronyms that were easy to remember and that stressed the points that they were trying to make.

I had some decisions before me. Did I really want this? Could I earn a living at it? There were so many things to be considered. If I did decide to become a professional speaker, I knew it would involve travelling. What about my children? How would they react to my being away from home, going out of town periodically? If I choose this as a career, I could set my own pace. One benefit was the wonderful feeling of being able to share part of myself with my audience. In turn, they opened up to me. I knew that life was giving and taking, and that's exactly what happened when I spoke. I gave myself to the audience and I wanted them to take what they needed in order to help them through some of their own rough spots. In turn, with their kind remarks and their comments on how I had helped, they were giving back to me. I wondered, isn't that what it's all about? Helping others. I could now use my own tragedy, that awful experience, and turn it into something good. It was a wonderful feeling knowing that I could possibly help other human beings overcome a seemingly insurmountable tragedy which may have been plaguing them. It is a wonderful feeling to be able to release those pent-up tragedies and put them into proper perspective. If I could help someone else through my own experiences. . . . I was definitely going to give it my whole-hearted effort. Insurance would wait.

CHAPTER NINE

Hard Work

As with my first talk, one presentation led to another. I was mainly limited to women's organizations for luncheon meetings which did not pay for my services. The luncheon talks were perfect. They got me out of the house in the afternoon. I was helping others, and it didn't take any time at all away from my family. I was unsure if this could be turned into a career. The need was definitely there, and I wanted to do my part. All people are faced with "trials and tribulations" in their daily lives. Too often we lose sight of what is really important in our lives. We spend too much time looking at what's wrong and too little on what we have done right. We spend a lot of time asking ourselves, "What if?" and not enough time asking, "What now?" We all have our problems; they started the moment we were born. It's how we handle those problems that makes us the individuals we are. The human spirit is very strong, but not everyone recognizes his or her own strength.

With every new audience came a new line of questions. Some wanted to know more about the man who had shot me and about the legal process. Some wanted to know more about my family. They wanted to know how my children handled the situation. They want to know about Wayne and our relationship. I took all these new questions home with me to think them through very carefully, because I could count on being asked them again by another audience. Each presentation set off a chain reaction, out of one talk would come another invitation and another and then another would follow. I found myself busy meeting many new people, touching their lives, sharing my story and giving them a different way of looking at their own lives. I answered all their questions as best I could. The answers came straight from the heart, straight-forward and honest. I started asking some questions of my own.

Since I had no difficulty in talking about or discussing the attack itself, I wanted to know more about the man who committed the crime. I wanted to know more about the legal process. I was literally kept in the dark during the trial. I was limited in what I knew to my own testimony, the closing arguments, the reading of the verdict, and the information that Wayne passed to me.

I asked Wayne if he would help me in obtaining more information about the trial. He could not understand why I wanted to pursue this and refused my request. I told him that it was important for me to have this information for my talks. Again he said he thought I was crazy and wanted no part of it. I knew if I was going to continue speaking, I was going to need this information. I was going to have to find a way to get things done. I always told my children, "There is a solution to every problem." I was going to find the solution. I called the prosecuting attorney, Mr. Garfield, and asked if I would be able to obtain a copy of Rossi's statement. He advised that he would arrange a time for me to come in and listen to the tapes. I had no difficulty in recruiting Chuck to drive me to Fort Lauderdale.

When we got there, we positioned the recorders so I could make a tape of the statement.

"Are you ready?" asked Chuck.

I took a deep breath. "I think so." I reached for both recorders and simultaneously pressed the buttons. I sat back in my chair making myself a little more comfortable. A deep male voice started. It was the unfamiliar voice of another detective, not Doug Haas as I had expected. This was the first recorded statement that Mr. Rossi had given the day he was apprehended. First the formalities took place. The detective had to read the rights and had a waiver agreement for Mr. Rossi to sign. He went over every point signed by Mr. Rossi. He was careful to state that no promises were made to Mr. Rossi nor was he paid any money nor was he under any pressure to give the statement. Mr. Rossi had to acknowledge each verbally. *"How formal, how proper, how careful law enforcement has to be. All the rights had to be read, his precious rights had to be preserved."* Then I heard that voice. It was slow, careful, and calculated. It was also so terrifyingly familiar. I was instantly thrown back to May 23rd, 1980. Out of the darkness came that same voice. Only this time I was seated safely in a room with Chuck by my side. I had to remind myself it was just a tape recording. Chuck must have seen me start to tremble the moment I heard Rossi. He pressed the button to stop the tape. Instantly I was brought back to reality.

"Are you all right?" Chuck asked.

I sat quietly for a moment to regain my composure, "Yes. You know,

Chuck, I forgot what he sounded like. For a whole year I hadn't heard his voice. I didn't even hear it during the trial. I really had forgotten what he sounded like. . . I want to hear the rest of it." Again I started the tapes.

Rossi continued with his version of that evening. He had started out in one of the local lounges where he was befriended by some people from out of town. He had been drinking rum. The people offered him some sort of pill, he said. He really didn't know what it was, but they told him it would just get him high. The police had thought it was a Quaalude. He told about how he left the parking lot and how he proceeded east down Federal Highway. There was a lull in the tape and Chuck spoke up, "That's funny, to the best of my knowledge Federal Highway only runs north and south in that area." I acknowledged Chuck's comment with a nod. Rossi continued. He told about how a car had spun out in front of him and he offered to assist the woman. He told the officer that there was no blood and that the woman really did not appear to be hurt. He told briefly how he drove me around and then took me to his apartment. He said that I agreed to have sex with him and that I had fallen on a knife.

The tape was finally over. I had to admit, he sounded convincing, but the evidence did not substantiate his story. I wondered what would have happened if the physical evidence would not have been so overwhelmingly in support of my statement. It was apparent throughout the statement that I was selected at random. Rossi had seen me as I was driving down the roadway. My God, I thought, it could have been any woman driving down that roadway. It could have been, but it wasn't. It was I: I had to live with it for the rest of my life. I was the one who had to choose a path for the rest of my life. I had to decide how I was going to use what life had dealt me. I gathered up my things with my thoughts running overtime. Chuck led me outside and over to Mr. Garfield's office where I returned the tapes. I thanked him and then asked how I could go about getting a copy of the court transcripts. The case was presently under appeal and all the transcripts had been sent to West Palm Beach to the Fourth District Court of Appeal. He gave me the name of the Assistant Attorney General who would be handling the case.

On the way home, Chuck and I discussed the present, what I was doing with my life today. I told him about the speaking. I told him about the questions and the personal stories.

"Give me a call the next time you speak. I would really like to hear you."

I felt slightly embarrassed that I was not first to extend the invitation for him to come and listen to one of my presentations. Somehow I felt he would be uninterested. I was delighted when he offered to come and listen. "You're on."

I kept trying to obtain a copy of the court transcripts. I phoned the number that Mr. Garfield provided. I gave the woman all the pertinent information that she needed to pull the records.

"The court transcript is over 1,000 pages. The cost to you will be twenty-five cents per page. Would you like me to place the order for you?"

"Twenty-five cents per page?" I asked. "That would be a minimum of $250.00."

"Probably a little over since, like I said, there's more than the 1,000 pages."

"Thank you very much, but that's all right. I don't think I can afford to get them right now. Could you please connect me with the Assistant Attorney General who will be handling the case?"

I was put on hold for a few moments and then a male voice inquired, "May I help you?"

"Yes, please, my name is Sharon Komlos, and I was the victim in the State versus Rossi."

"Yes, Mrs. Komlos, Mr. Garfield told me you might be calling. He said something about a copy of the court transcripts. The appeal is set to be heard February 1st of 1982. You could probably get a copy of it after the hearing."

"There is one problem. The young lady on the phone told me it could cost twenty-five cents a page; that's over $250.00."

"Yes, that's a lot of money. And you know something, the criminal in prison receives a copy of these transcripts free of charge. He gets them because of his appeal."

I couldn't believe what I was hearing. The criminal receives them free and I, the victim, have to pay twenty-five cents a page. Haven't I paid enough? It was not fair. "This just doesn't seem right. First I was not allowed to sit in the courtroom and listen to the proceedings and now, if I want to obtain a copy of the transcripts, I have to pay for them. I really would like them, but I just cannot afford them at this time. I have other things to be concerned with like food and clothing for my children. I know this is something that Mr. Rossi does not have to concern himself with while in prison. Isn't it something, he gets everything provided for him while in prison, and I am still paying."

I really did not mean to direct my anger at the gentleman on the other end of the phone, but I had to speak what I felt. "Well, thank you any-way for your help. Will you please advise me of the outcome of the appeal. Naturally, I'm interested."

"Of course, Mrs. Komlos, I will let you know." I knew he could feel the frustration in my voice. But rules are rules, and procedures are procedures, and I could understand that he was doing his job. I was justly upset. If it were not for me, there would have been no trial, and thus, no transcripts in the first place. What happened to, "Equal justice under the law?"

I decided that my next source for information would be Wayne. After all, he was victimized as well. I also felt it was about time that we discussed what happened more openly. This might be the therapy that he needed. I never really did get all the details about what happened in the household while I was lying there in Rossi's apartment. I knew I would get the answers only if I asked the questions point blank. I wanted to know how he was notified, what his feelings were. We had discussed this briefly last June. Enough time had elapsed, and now we should be able to discuss it in depth. Wayne told me that the police knocked on the door at 4:00 o'clock in the morning and notified him that his vehicle had been involved in a shooting, but that I was not found. He remembered calling my mother in Ohio to find out exactly what hotel Tammy was staying in so the police could contact her. He told me about looking at the car at the police pound. The front seat was covered with blood and the passenger side window was broken. There was a large hole cut in the right front side of the roof where the police had dug out a bullet that lodged in the roof rail of the car. The interior of the car was covered with a fine black powder that the police used for dusting for fingerprints. He said all morning he wondered and worried where I was. He drove down the roads near the canal along the two-lane highway I would have taken home, hoping to find a sign to lead to my whereabouts. He remembered getting nauseous from the sights and the smell of the car while driving it home from the police pound. He told me that Shawn snuck into the garage after he had told him not to. Shawn's curiosity got the best of him. He told me about the telephone call he received at 12:00 o'clock in the afternoon informing him that I was in Broward General Hospital. The woman from the Rape Crisis Center told him that I was in the emergency room, but that I was fine. He remembered the sight of me laying on the gurney with my eyes as black as two handballs and blood covering me from head to toe. He told me that he picked my parents up at the airport and brought them to the hospital while I was in Intensive Care. I told Wayne that I remembered that as a dream-like situation.

Wayne recapped the incident mechanically. He made it seem as though it were just a story from years ago and had no particular significance. I knew it meant much more than that. We were all devastated by the experience. It hurt everyone. We were all victims: Me, Wayne, the children, my parents.

My inquiries continued. I called and spoke with Doug Haas, one of the investigating detectives on the case. I wanted to know more about how they found Rossi. He said that Charlie Greenwood, who found me screaming on the balcony, had told the police the exact location of the balcony. The police obtained the necessary warrants and went back to the apartment, but by the time they returned, the apartment had already been cleaned. It was apparent that Rossi returned, found me gone, and fled. He turned the mattress over and made the bed. When the police started investigating, they checked the underside of the mattress and found the bloodstains. They checked for some of the articles which I told them about—the remote control for the television, the tight piece of cloth over the walls, the louvered doors. They found my fingerprints on the walls. They knew they had the right place. Detective Haas called the telephone numbers in a personal telephone book they found. At each number he asked for Tommy. He finally reached a telephone number where the male at the other end told him that Tommy was asleep and asked if he wanted him awakened. Detective Haas said no, that he'd call back later. The police ran a trace on the telephone number and found that it was assigned to a residence in North Miami Beach. The Fort Lauderdale police then contacted North Miami Beach to stake out the apartment complex. They apprehended Rossi as he was running through a wooded area with the plastic trashbag containing my clothing. With the proper warrants in order, they then searched his car. Willingly he was brought back to the Fort Lauderdale Police Department.

We talked briefly about our legal system. The police were closely scrutinized both during the investigation and during the trial. They had to be very careful to do everything right, not to violate the rights of the criminal. His rights were guaranteed by the Constitution and protected under the law. Rossi knew the law, he knew his rights, and he knew that he was protected. This was not his first bout with the criminal justice system. I asked Doug what really happened with Rossi's first case. He was originally sentenced to a brief term in prison for the 1970 assault on that young woman in New York. He really brutalized her. She was stabbed, raped and left for dead. She suffered serious psychological trauma. Rossi served a portion of his sentence for that crime before he was released on parole. He came out of prison and assaulted a second young woman in the back seat of his car. The second woman did not want to prosecute for her own personal reasons. He was then put back into prison for parole violation, to serve out his sentence. He emerged a free man and moved to Florida. He lived in the Fort Lauderdale area for approximately a year before he attacked me.

Detective Haas filled in some of the gaps for me. No one could answer all of my remaining questions. What was Rossi doing out, a free man, on the streets in the first place? Why didn't someone recognize a long time ago that he needed help? There was no doubt in my mind that there was something terribly wrong with him? How far back did his problem go? Did it start with his childhood? What would ever lead him to treat another human being the way that he had?

I was more than pleased when asked to speak for the Broward County Anti-Crime Conference. I was to be one of the seven keynote speakers and was scheduled to speak last. I had my fourteen minute presentation down pat. My inquiries and preparation were about to be put to use.

"I'm a 1980 statistic for Broward County. I never expected to be a victim of a crime, but I was." I continued telling my story of the night of the attack. "There is a desperate need for people to get involved. A conference such as this one is important. But don't just let it die right here. The effects must be far-reaching. People need to be educated and realize that the hand of crime can reach out and strike anyone at any time. It doesn't care what you look like or who you are, it doesn't care where you live or how much money you earn. A violent crime is not just something you read about in the newspaper or watch on television on the news at six or eleven. It's real and it reaches everyone. Everyone is exposed by virtue of being a human being on the face of this earth. People in number can make a difference. It's up to you."

I stood at the lectern waiting for someone to help me back to my chair. The applause increased. I could hear the noise rise. Someone came up to me to assist me back to my chair and whispered in my ear. "They're giving you a standing ovation."

At this conference I received coverage on the news broadcasts and in the local newspapers for the first time as Sharon Komlos, a woman who was now taking control of her life and trying to make people aware, rather than as a nameless victim.

I started to keep records of my speaking engagements on my mini tape recorder. The calendar was filling up fast. I was excited and enthusiastic. I was asked to speak at a Methodist church in Fort Lauderdale. It was a fellowship dinner and the family was invited. I had told the children what I had been doing, but they only knew that I was speaking to other people. They really didn't know what it involved; now was their chance to hear me. I told Wayne about the dinner and that everyone was invited. I felt it would be a good opportunity for him to hear me as well. I was hurt, but not really surprised by his reply. He told me at the beginning that he never wanted to hear me speak, that he felt I was crazy, and he just didn't want to get involved. He now told me I could go alone. There was no way I was going to drag him to something like that. He never heard me speak, and he never wanted to. He made his feelings very clear. He wanted me to cancel the engagement and told me he would not watch the children. I couldn't help being angry. I wondered if this was how it was going to be every time I was asked to speak. I considered calling off the engagement, but only for a second. I told him that he would not have to watch the children; I would take them with me. I still had plenty of time to make arrangements. I called Chuck, remembering what he had said previously about wanting to hear me speak. He was more than delighted.

The fellowship dinner presentation went well. The children were proud of their mother, especially when I introduced them to the audience and praised them for their courage and their strength in overcoming adversity. They were wonderful children, and naturally I was a proud mother. I introduced Chuck as a friend, someone who was there when I needed him. My ex-boss from the insurance company along with one of the secretaries also attended the dinner. They came along to critique my new career. After the presentation, the usual question and answer period followed. Once again, there were the predictable questions. "Did you go through a long period of depression?" was the first one. Once again I repeated my answers, "That deep dark depression never did really take a good foothold. I decided I had too much to do with my life to spend all that time being depressed."

The questioning turned to the criminal. Had he been apprehended and sentenced? Would he ever get out? I was glad I had prepared because now I had the answers. The line of questioning turned to my family. People remarked that the children appeared to be taking everything in stride. I told the audience that my children were normal. They had their moments, but what children didn't. At times there were trying moments in the household, but we worked them through together. One woman in the back of the room asked about my husband and why he wasn't with us tonight. For the very first time, I was not honest with my audience. I made up the excuse that he was busy and unable to attend. I explained to her that there are always victims in a crime, that my husband was victimized as well as my children and my parents. All of them felt the effects of the crime. I hold her that naturally, it was quite a shock for him, and that he was handling it in the way that was right for him. I was unable to elaborate any further. I thanked the audience for listening and once again closed to a round of applause. Chuck helped me down off the stage and over to the children. Kristin complained that she was tired and wanted to go home. The boys were just a little more patient. My ex-boss, Kevin, congratulated me on a job well done, "Not bad for an ex-adjuster. You're doing great, keep up the fabulous work."

The children monopolized most of the conversation on the way home. I was not my usual talkative self. I told Chuck I was all talked out, but he knew there was more. When we arrived home, I sent the children off to their rooms to get ready for bed.

"All right, Sharon, what's wrong?"

I couldn't keep it to myself any longer, I couldn't hold back the tears. "Wayne and I have separated."

CHAPTER TEN

A Single Mother

For months Wayne and I had an in-house separation. By November of 1981 the divorce papers had been filed and Wayne moved out. I was living alone with three children I could not see.

Even though the children were all very young, they all knew what the word "divorce" meant. Shawn was now ten, Marc was nine, and Kristin was four. I explained to them that it was not going to be easy, but together we would make it. Not all of our times were good. We laughed together and cried together. We shared each other's frustrations and worked out our difficulties. I told the children that we could find a solution to any problem. And I swear that they would lie awake at night creating new problems for me to solve.

Our major difficulty was transportation. We relied on neighbors, Chuck, and a local taxicab service for rides wherever we wanted to go. I would usually go grocery shopping with a neighbor or with Chuck. I recall one Saturday morning when we ran out of milk, ice cream, cookies, and some of the more essential foods needed for the children. My neighbors were not available for a ride, and I did not feel it was necessary to call Chuck for something as minor as just a few items from the local grocery store. My children stood by patiently waiting for me to find a solution. I called for a taxi and told the children to get ready. In the cab, I questioned my sanity for allowing myself to be led around a grocery store by three small children. I felt it would be a good way to show them that I trusted them with every step I took. They were to be my eyes, and they didn't seem to mind the challenge. The taxicab driver seemed quite amused that any mother, much less a blind mother, would brave a trip to the grocery store with three small children. He asked, "Are you sure you are going to be all right?" I assured him that the children were very good at leading me around. They had done it numerous times before. The taxi stopped, and the boys opened the door. Very gently,

Kristin reached for my hand to lead me out of the taxi. Once again the taxi driver asked, "Are you really sure you are going to be all right?" as he watched me exiting from his cab. I started to reply, not really paying attention to where I was going, following Kristin who was not really paying attention to where she was leading me, "Yes, I'm quite sure we're going to be all right," I said as Kristin led me right into one of the concrete columns in front of the grocery store.

"Oops, sorry mom," Kristin said apologetically as she hurried me around the concrete pole. I could just imagine what that taxicab driver was thinking as he sat in his cab watching the children hurry me through the door. I arranged with the children that I would stand behind the cart appearing to push while the boys would pull the cart in front. Shawn naturally wanted to lead since he was the oldest. Marc put up only a slight argument but then conceded that they would share the responsibility. Kristin wanted to sit in the child seat and then wanted to walk and then wanted to sit back in the child seat and then again wanted to walk; I made the final decision that she would walk and could also help me push the cart. The children rushed me very quickly past the fresh fruits and vegetables. They managed to find the milk and some orange juice, but were adamant that they could not find the meat counter. Kristin picked out her favorite breakfast cereal and then found another and another. I finally limited her to one box. The cookie aisle was Kristin's favorite. She had difficulty deciding on the brand of chocolate chip cookies. While Kristin decided, the boys took off to the other side of the aisle to find more items we needed. I could hear the noises of the items being tossed into the shopping cart. Kristin advised me that her selection was made, and the cookies were in the cart.

"Well, children, let's head for the checkout," I said to my young trio. I thought the little shopping spree had gone relatively well. While we were standing in the checkout line, I gave Shawn a quarter and a telephone number for the taxi. Kristin assisted me in unloading the grocery cart while Marc supervised. The cashier, Sally, knew me from my weekly visits. She was a little surprised that I ventured out alone with the children. "My you are brave today, Sharon, aren't you?" she said with a slight laugh in her voice. Shawn returned with the news that his task had been completed, and the taxi would be here shortly.

"Sharon, now I know you are a good mother with nutrition in mind, but don't you think ten packages of chocolate chip cookies is going a bit far?"

"Kristin!" I said knowing full well who the culprit was. I told Sally that two bags would be sufficient. Kristin did not object.

The transition from a two-parent to a one-parent household went remarkably smoothly and was a little easier than I expected. The daytime schedule remained pretty much the same; after all Wayne worked when he was living at home, and the children were in school during the day. It was during the evening hours that some changes took place. Assisting with homework did not pose any difficulties. The boys helped one another, and if they were stumped by a question turned to me for an answer. We found that with a little added patience, we could work out any problems. The boys assisted me in reading the mail. They even learned how to write out simple checks. My checkbook was specially designed for the blind. It had raised lines which I could feel. I told the boys what needed to be entered on what particular line. The more difficult tasks were left for an adult, usually Chuck. It didn't take long for the children to recognize that we were able to make it on our own. The key words always seemed to be sensitivity, patience, and communication. Whatever we did, or whatever problem arose, as long as we were sensitive to each other's feelings and each other's needs, as long as we had the patience with one another and communicated our feelings and talked about the problem, we always managed to find a solution.

It was only during the evening hours, the time after the children had gone to bed and I was left alone that the reality of the dissolution of an eleven-year marriage entered my thoughts. For those eleven years I had always had the presence of a man—not necessarily someone to depend upon totally, but at least someone to share the good times and the bad. I wondered when that sharing stopped. I really wondered if there was still any love left for either of us. When and how did it change? We must have been in love in the beginning. It was so long ago. We were both rather young, I was only twenty when we were married and a year older when I had Shawn. Very soon this eleven-year marriage would be a part of my past, just as the shooting and the trial had become. I thank God for three of His miracles that the marriage had produced—my loving, wonderful children. I knew I could not think for Wayne or be responsible for him. I knew that once the divorce was finalized, I would be out of his life forever. There was relief in knowing that Wayne agreed the children should remain in my custody. There had also been a sense of relief within the household itself. Gone were the tensions, the anticipated arguments, the continuous fighting about anything and everything. I much preferred solitude to constant confrontations. The evenings were quiet, and that was an improvement.

Now, more than ever, it was necessary to have my mind clearly set on a career. The children would not stay young forever, I knew as they grew so would my need for a better income. Even now the expenses seemed to consume everything.

My mother decided it might be a good idea for a trip to Florida to visit her grandchildren and her daughter, who just might be able to use her help. The first order of business was changing the payee on my social security checks. Immediately after I was shot, Wayne had filed the papers with social security disability. He decided it would be easier to handle the check if he were named as payee. I agreed and signed the necessary papers naming him instead of me as the payee. Now my mother could say, "I told you so," because she was against that arrangement. I hoped I could handle the whole matter over the telephone but found the problem could only be rectified in person. We borrowed a car from a friend, and I gave my mother directions to the closest social security office. I anticipated long lines and lengthy waits but much to my surprise, we were taken immediately and introduced to our case worker. She sat quietly listening to my request, "I was told by your tele-answering service that I had to make the request in person. I would like to change the payee on my checks. At the present time, my husband's name appears as the payee on my social security checks as well as those for my children. We are currently going through a divorce, and he has moved out of the house. It is increasingly difficult to have him endorse the checks every month. I would like to have the checks with me as the payee."

"Are the children receiving the checks under your social security or your husband's?"

"The children receive it under mine." There was silence at the desk as the young woman reviewed her file.

"Well, Mrs. Komlos, first of all you will have to obtain a letter from a psychologist stating that you are fully capable of handling you own finances. There had to be a reason for the checks being put in your husband's name, which only tells me that you are incapable of handling your finances. I cannot change them for you just like that."

I could not believe what I was hearing, "I am fully capable of handling my own finances. The only reason it was initially made out to my husband was because he felt it would be easier for him since I am totally blind and he did all of the banking. I did not need a psychologist's evaluation when I signed the papers making him the payee. I don't understand why I would need one now."

My mother intervened, "She doesn't even have a psychologist. All she had was an eye doctor and she doesn't even need him anymore. Who is going to pay for this evaluation? Are you?"

The young woman stood her ground, "No, ma'am, we do not pay for psychologist evaluations. There is nothing I can do, I will not change the checks unless you have that letter from a psychologist."

It was becoming increasingly apparent that we were making no headway with this young woman. Usually I abide by the rules and do not like to cause a scene. It was bad enough I had to wait a full five months to receive my first social security check to prove that my disability was permanent even thought there were doctors' statements affirming my sight would never be recovered. This time it was a matter of principle. "You have my file right in front of you, I'm sure you can see for yourself that there was no psychologist report stating that I am incapable of handling my own finances. I signed a paper making my husband payee for my checks and the children immediately upon my release from the hospital. It was a rather traumatic time for all of us and anything that would make the situation easier I agreed to. And this is my payment? Let me tell you about what happened." I proceeded to tell the young woman about the night that took my sight and the reason for me receiving the social security checks in the first place. I was careful not to leave out any of the gruesome details. "And now my husband and I have separated and are going through a divorce. I'm alone with my children and it is almost impossible to have him endorse the checks every month. I'm quite positive an exception is in order here."

Tearfully the young woman agreed. Quickly she left the desk and then returned, "I just received my supervisor's approval. I can only understand a little of what you are going through. I am divorced and trying to raise two children of my own. I'm sorry." She guaranteed me that the paperwork would be filed and the correction on the checks should be made by my January check. She gave me her name and telephone number if I should have any other questions or problems. I thanked her for her assistance and my mother led me out.

On the way home my mother and I discussed red tape and bureaucracy. I was amazed how they could take something so simple and turn it into something so difficult. This whole experience gave a new dimension to the phrase, "Adding insult to injury." It was just another of the minor gnawing irritations of life. Previously, I never dealt with the social welfare system because I never needed their services. There was nothing like a firsthand experience with bureaucratic red tape to make me confront the problems. With all of their red tape there is no way they could be cost effective. I felt the same frustration with the social security system as I had with the Division of Blind Services. It was frustrating to need their services in the first place, but then to be treated as though I had no mind of my own was infuriating. Blindness did not keep me down and it was going to take more than the social welfare agencies to bring me to my knees. I was gaining "expertise" in the art of problem solving. They provided more material for my presentations and added a touch of humor.

I should have known that the Social Security Administration was totally incapable of solving the problem at one stroke. The checks arrived in January just as always before—made out to Wayne as payee. I called three times in February to try to get the situation remedied. Twice, caseworkers promised to call me back; both failed. The third called back and told me that the February checks would be made out to me as payee. In February, they made out one of the checks to me. They made out a second to Wayne. They did not send the third check. I called and was told that one of my children must have turned eighteen. When I protested that this was not the case, I was told that Wayne had taken custody of one of the children. When I objected that this was not the case, the caseworker conceded that there might just be a problem. I was promised a correction in March.

The March checks all arrived—all made out to Wayne. Once again I got on the telephone. In April, one of the checks was made out to me and the other two to Wayne. Again I called Social Security, whose number I knew by heart by now. And I kept calling. Finally, a man told me that the situation was becoming ridiculous. Anyone but a welfare worker would have reached that conclusion in February. At any rate, he told me the problem was a bug in the computer program which made it impossible to enter the changes without reprogramming. A programmer would have to take care of it, and that would take two months. Apparently, he was correct, because in June the correct amount of money arrived in two checks both made out to me as payee.

CHAPTER ELEVEN

Gains As A Speaker

As I spoke more, I began to meet seasoned, professional speakers. I found that there were different methods of marketing, and a rather lengthy list of "dos and don'ts" of the speaking profession. Some suggestions included joining various speakers' organizations, the network of fellow speakers which could assist me in my new profession. Other suggestions were to get an expensive but necessary brochure, and the services of an agent or a booking bureau for speakers.

I quickly learned that I was a novice in this interesting and highly competitive profession. Paradoxically, I found that I could not get hired for pay unless I was heard, and I could not get heard unless I was hired. I wanted to establish my own guidelines. If was going to take a little longer than the norm, that was how it would have to be. I was not ready for an expensive brochure, mass marketing, or an agent. I would not travel seven days a week at the expense of my children. I prized my sanity. I could not see what value my experiences would be to anyone if I talked about taking control of one's life, about doing what was right for one as an individual but I lost that control and individuality by conforming to the guidelines that had been right for other speakers. My situation was much different from theirs. I was a single parent. Since my children almost lost me once, I did not want them to feel that they were losing me again to a career. I felt it best to ease us into a new profession. I wanted to gain expertise in speaking techniques, and I wanted to feel comfortable in front of an audience.

I had been assured by veteran speakers that it was possible to earn a good income from the circuit. It would not come easy. The pace was hectic, and only the best were able to earn enough to support a family on the fees. I wanted to be one of the best. I made the commitment. Nonetheless, the touchstone would always be, "What is best for my children?" and never, "What is best for my speaking career?"

Immediately, I found obstacles in my pursuit of a speaking career: The preconceived notions that people had. First, I was a woman, supposedly frailer than my male counterparts. Then, I was considered rather young from the standpoint of being a motivational, inspirational platform speaker. The title, "Wise Old Sage," complete with all of his vast, worldly knowledge on the topics of motivation and philosophy did not apply to a blond in her thirties. Finally, there was my blindness. This, somehow, placed me in a category of being more frail and fragile than just being a woman. It was believed by the majority of people who were booking speakers that since I did not have sight I would be unable to travel long distances, stay in hotels alone, or would collapse with the frantic pace of speaking. The only real limitations I had were placed on me by other people. They had preconceived limitations in mind. I already knew that the most difficult obstacles to overcome were those lurking in the minds of others. This was definitely going to be a challenge, and I loved it.

I had no difficulty obtaining unpaid speaking engagements for the local women's organizations. I looked at these as learning experiences, both in refining speaking skills and in obtaining exposure. They enabled me quickly to gather a portfolio of personal letters of commendation from people who heard me speak to their organizations.

After the article by Dr. Dyer in *Family Circle* magazine hit the newsstands, I was asked to be on some local television as well as national television shows, thus gaining more exposure and new insight into working with the media. More television, radio and newspaper interviews followed. More exposure. Every time I mentioned the word "exposure" to my mother, her reply was, "You cannot put exposure in the bank." More than just the exposure and the experience, I was finding an increasing insight into human nature. The personal experiences of others had been shared with me time and time again and reconfirmed that I was pursuing the right career. I just could not explain to my mother or anyone else the wonderful feeling that came during the one-on-one conversations after a presentation. I helped one woman who had just gone through the pain of losing a child. I helped a young woman overcome divorce and another to shed the guilt because she was a working mother; the stories went on and on—everything from victims of crime to people who had a difficult time in overcoming the trials of day-to-day life. I stressed repeatedly that I did not want people to change their lives to conform to mine, rather I wanted to offer them alternative ways of thinking which might assist them in overcoming obstacles to their success. It was a wonderful feeling to know that I was doing something beneficial. I was

SHARON KOMLOS

130

using my experience to help others.

The majority of my audiences were women. There were only a few occasions where I had spoken to mixed audiences; women's organizations seemed most interested in my story. A man wanted me to speak to his male organization. The meeting planner, a woman, objected, saying, "Appropriate for the women's organizations but I don't see how she could carry an all-male audience." Naturally, I was shocked. I had felt some prejudice against women in the workplace prior to the loss of my sight; it never stopped me before. Because the prejudice was now verbalized by a woman, I knew the attitude existed more universally. I did not want to be looked upon as strictly a woman speaker. I had a message for everyone, and I wanted everyone to hear me.

I received a telephone call from a woman who was substitute teaching at Fort Lauderdale High School. "Hi, my name is Karen Leach. I heard you speak a while back at the college, for the Anti-Crime Conference. I thought you were absolutely fantastic. I am subbing for a psychology teacher at the high school, and I would like you to speak to my students. I know that you are accustomed to receiving a fee, but I don't have any money. The best I could do for you is supply you lunch and give you free transportation." She paused for a moment. I thought to myself, here we go again, no fee, high school students. There was definitely a need, and it would be a new audience. I listened as she continued, "I am not quite sure about the date. It would have to be set according to your schedule, naturally. I will pick you up at six o'clock in the morning and I have five classes. After the last class I can return you home. I feel it is very necessary for the students to hear your story. I know that you could be a great help to them, especially with today's peer pressures and the stress experienced in growing up."

Again I thought silently, five hours, six o'clock in the morning. "Yes, I'd be delighted."

It was not easy getting up at five o'clock a.m. to be ready for my ride at six. The first class started at seven a.m. I had the full class period. This was going to be a challenge in more ways than one. First, I had to keep a class of bleary-eyed high school students awake. I wasn't quite sure how they would receive a woman older than thirty. After all, during my own high school years the saying was, "Don't trust anyone over thirty!" I knew that high school students could not be fooled; they size you up in a moment. Their short attention span wouldn't last longer than my introduction if they thought my topic uninteresting. If I could get through, if I could make them understand that strength comes from within and not from an outside source, if I could help them to understand that they are the ones controlling, steering their lives, I then would be accomplishing my goal. I decided to take the only approach I knew: Be straightforward and honest. After all, I was going to have five tries, five presentations in a row, each forty-five minutes long. How was I going to make the fifth presentation as exciting and fresh as the first?

That morning, as usual, I began speaking about the facts of my life: Origins, family, and career. I told them about setting a goal for myself and how I had attained it and how life was wonderful. I went on to the attack that changed my life. I talked about the attitudes and ideas that other people had for me, like the Division of Blind Services. I talked about the difficulties in getting started all over again and my new set of goals.

"The road to your ultimate goal is not always straight and narrow; life takes diversions, and often new goals surface. Life is not always easy, and the earlier you learn that, the better off you are going to be. It takes a lot of perseverance, determination, and downright hard work." I was sure I was not telling them anything they hadn't heard before, but this time I was telling them from my own personal experience. "No one would have blamed me if I had decided to go into a closet and hide for the rest of my life. No one would have blamed me if I decided to remain angry and keep all that anger and frustration and self-pity locked up inside. No one, no one would have blamed me at all. There's only one person with whom I have to be happy. There's only one person who I have to live with and that is myself. If you experienced some tragedy whether it be major or even minor in your own lifetime, you know how you reacted to it. My belief is that mine is over and done with and if I keep a lot of useless emotion locked up inside of me, it is giving the man who took my eyesight and ten hours of my life a lot more time than he deserves. He has already taken enough. I am not going to give him one moment more."

These words were spoken with strength and conviction and received a burst of applause from my young audience. I was really getting through.

"There were some people who told me that I did not react normally to the situation. I felt I was perfectly normal. I was reacting to the situation the only way that I knew how. I really wanted to know who set forth those guidelines for normal. If overcoming adversity and being happy with your life is abnormal, then I'll take it. That night of the attack is in the past. And I'm not setting my sights so far ahead in the future that I forget about today. I found out if I take care of today, tomorrow is going to be just fine. Let me close with this one last thought for you to think about applying to your daily living. When you look at the past, just give it a glance and wave it good-bye; when you look to the future, greet it with the hopes of only good things to come. But when you look at the present, the todays in which we live, look at it as through the eyes of a small child, complete with all its wonder, amazement, excitement and enthusiasm. But more than just looking at it, live it, experience each and every one of these todays. They are just too important to waste."

I ended my presentation to a round of applause and then a standing ovation from the students in the room. Unknown to me then, a few teachers were present. I stood there for a moment clearing my throat and just thinking, I had found a new audience. They were young and had their whole lives ahead of them. I hoped that I contributed something positive to their lives. I had a feeling that I did.

We had only a few moments left for questions, and they came quickly. During my presentation I had forgotten totally about the man who had assaulted me. The first line of questioning was about him, just where he was, how much time he was serving and why he was out there in the first place. I was quick to advise my audience that I was not allowed in the courtroom during the trial, therefore, my knowledge was from what other people told me. Another burst of applause came when I told the young students that this man was serving a term of 104 years in the State Prison. The students asked about my personal life, "Are you going through the divorce because of what has happened to you?"

"I'll answer that the only way I can. I'm not quite sure. If you were to ask that question of my husband today, he would say that it was coming for a long time, but I just don't know. To me it will be something that will remain unknown. But it did happen, it's a fact and reality. The divorce should be finalized soon. It is something that happened and, like it or not, we have to go on."

The next question was from a young man, "Since you are going through the divorce, the next time around, what kind of a man are you looking for?"

"Why? Do you have a father you would like to give away," A burst of laughter came from the audience. "Really, I'm not quite sure because I'm not looking. If, and when, I am ready to get involved with another man, he would have to be somebody who will accept me for what and who I am. He will have to be someone who will not want to change me. In turn, I will accept him for who he is and I will not try to change him. We will have to have a relationship based on mutual respect, trust and desire for each other. I'm basically a romantic at heart. I really like all the sweet, wonderful, mushy things that romantic love brings."

Karen whispered in my ear, "Boy are you looking for someone who doesn't exist."

The bell rang, putting an end to the questions. Some of the students stopped by to say thank you and just to shake my hand. I reached out and touched a young frail hand of a girl. Her soft voice spoke up, "Sharon, you have no idea how much you have helped me. I'm only fourteen years old, but I was raped a year ago. It is something I never quite dealt with, and I never did report it to the police. I haven't even told my mother or anyone except for my best friend. I never felt that anyone would understand. It was a horrible experience, not as bad as you went through, but I know that you know what it felt like. You have helped me so much, you'll never know just how much. I had to come up and say thank you. I just wished I had heard you a year ago."

Unashamed, the young girl reached out and give me a big hug. I felt that any words that I would speak now would be inadequate, "Thank you for sharing that with me, I think you'll be just fine." How horrifying, I thought, but how true, how real.

I never knew who was going to be in my audience or what they had experienced. Yes, there was a definite need.

The other four classes were just as attentive and excited as the first. Karen vowed that there was a need for other schools in the area to hear me speak and considered it her mission to find a way for me to speak to all of them. I had found a new audience who were young, excited, vibrant, often confused, subjected to stress, peer pressure, and drugs. They were at a very impressionable age. I wanted to leave them with my thoughts and beliefs. I wanted them to understand that they contained within themselves the power to be successful. I didn't want them to blame others for their failure. There were plenty of copouts. They had to understand that they had to make the best choices possible for themselves and that no one could give them the answers. I stressed individual perseverance, and determination. I hoped that hearing me speak would influence their lives positively. At least they truly heard me.

I needed all the perseverance and determination I could muster to keep pace with my mounting problems. My mother stayed through much of December. She wanted to keep an eye on Wayne as he removed his personal belongings from the house. She wanted to be sure that he did not take what belonged to me. It was not yet agreed how much money Wayne was to pay in child support or alimony. My finances were dwindling; everything we had saved had gone into furnishing our new home and paying off some outstanding debts. And Christmas was coming with its expenses.

It was mid-December when I received a letter from the Crimes Compensation Board for the State of Florida. "Oh, good, that must be the check, the one that Shelly told me about. She told me there would be no difficulty..." There was only silence when my mother opened the letter; she interrupted me right in the middle of my sentence.

"Don't get your hopes up yet, Sharon, there is no check enclosed."

The Crimes Compensation Board informed me that I had not suffered "serious financial hardship" according to their definition. It was for that reason that I did not conform to the section of the code that would have provided financial assistance. They had turned me down, flat. There would be no compensation at all. It was not what I had expected.

"How could they possibly say I did not suffer serious financial hardship? I don't understand it. First I get shot, kidnapped, stabbed, raped and I'm left for dead. I lose my eyesight. Can anyone ever put a price on eyesight? And now the divorce. I lose my job, then my husband, what next?"

"Try and calm down. Maybe you can appeal this."

I just couldn't understand their reasoning, as hard as I tried. I was penalized for being a working woman. Through my job I had the proper health insurance. I tried to make my own way. Sure I had the support of my husband in the beginning but who knew what was going to happen now in going through the divorce? It seemed as though crimes compensation for the state only covered the medical bills that were outstanding as a result of a person not having health insurance. There were no provisions for being totally and permanently disabled as the result of being a victim of a violent or serious crime. An appeal would take an attorney, and an attorney would cost money. The maximum amount of the award I could receive would be $10,000. I knew that they had all the facts. They knew that I was totally blind and knew that I was unable to return to work. They had all of those facts during their investigation, and it was highly unlikely that they would reverse their decision. I decided to let it drop and worry about what I could control.

It was going to take an awful lot of perseverance and determination to make the speaking work. I was not going to give up on that.

As the weeks went by, new routines at home became established. At the first mention of a divorce, the children thought that they were losing their father. It took a little time until the routine was really established. Their weekdays were spent with me and their weekends with their father.

Very quickly they learned that they could not have the ideal world of having us together. They understood that they did not lose their father and they definitely had their mother. They were very comfortable in knowing that the custody would remain with me and that their father would have visitation rights.

Wayne, however, was not satisfied. It was a Saturday afternoon when he came to pick up the children, "I've come to a decision," he said in a very stern, abrupt voice. "I'm going to fight you on the custody for the children; I also want you out of the house. I already notified my attorney. I want the kids and the house."

At first I just stood there in disbelief. Then I could feel the outrage mounting, "Why? I thought the custody and the house were already settled, you already agreed to both. Why now? Why the change all of a sudden?"

For the first time I was losing my composure, really, truly, losing it. I was so outraged that I started to cry uncontrollably. Just the thought of a custody battle was upsetting. The house was a material object. I could always find another place to live. But the children, what reasons could he possibly have for wanting to take them?

He just stood at the front door watching me as I cried. He didn't have the decency to leave. I felt that he actually enjoyed this sight; I, who had been strong for so long, broken at the threat of losing my children. It would be a terrible loss. He could come over and see them whenever he wanted. He had the flexibility and mobility of using a car; I did not. I would literally be at his mercy. From what was going on now, I felt that he would not be at all merciful.

"I can't believe you are doing this. I just can't believe it. This was already agreed upon. You said there would be no problem, I could keep the children. You wouldn't put us through a custody battle. You know, Wayne, what Rossi did was one thing. It was over and done with very quickly. It was easily resolved, but what you're doing is totally inexcusable. It's been almost a year already, and we have been back and forth so many times. When is it ever going to end? You really seem to enjoy making things more difficult than they should be. I just don't understand it. I am going to fight you, Wayne! I am going to fight you all the way down the line! Naturally I want what is best for the children, but the best in this case is for them to stay with me, not you! I'll have proof and plenty of it! But I'll fight you all the way down the line! Now will you please get out of my house!"

In a very calm and a matter-of-fact voice he said as he walked towards the door, "I'll bring them back at nine o'clock," and he closed the door behind him. I stood there, holding onto the door handle, listening for the engine to start up and then fade into the distance. I stood there, still crying, wondering what happened. Talk about overcoming, about perseverance and determination, about being strong and overcoming adversity. My God, I thought, it's not easy, especially when something like this happens. Why does he have to make it so much harder than it need be? The emotional ups and downs are very difficult to handle. It is one thing when you know in which direction you are going, but it is something else entirely when someone else changes his course and yours.

I walked over to my chair and sat down. *"Think, Sharon, think this whole thing through. It is a weekend and I cannot call my attorney. I will give him a call first thing Monday morning. Now I know which way Wayne is headed. He wants the house and the children. I'm going to fight for both. I'll just tell the attorney. Again I am going to have to prepare myself mentally for another battle. At least I have some previous experience, it isn't the first time, and I know it isn't going to be the last."*

With divorce and a custody fight looming, I became sensitive to and heard more about these problems from other people. One night Mary and I got together over a bottle of wine to commiserate. Mary was soon to be divorced and had custody of her three children. Our situations were only a little different, but we both knew the turmoil of divorce.

"You know, it's amazing to me how two supposedly logical, full-grown adults can be diminished to arguing, pettiness, and bickering over property settlements and how much the father is going to pay to support his children."

Mary jumped in, "Why should the divorce be any easier than the marriage?"

"You know, we've been married for eleven years. I guess that doesn't count for anything. For those eleven years we used to be able to discuss our problems up until two years ago. Then everything seems to have broken down totally."

"Sharon, divorce is never easy. Mine has been going on even longer than yours has. Now, look at me. I really don't want to spend the rest of my life alone, I enjoy the company of a man, but what man in his right mind is going to get involved with a woman with three children, and let's face it, I'm not in the most desirable category. I'm already thirty. The men out there are looking for someone younger. So here I am, thirty and with three children. That's really depressing."

I sat there quietly thinking about what Mary had said, looking at her situation and then looking at mine. I'm already over thirty—thirty-two to be exact, and I also have three children. And to top off everything else off, I'm totally blind. If she felt that her odds were really slim in finding another man, what were mine? I spent the evening thinking about an awful lot.

The substitute teacher who arranged my first talk at Fort Lauderdale High School, Karen Leach, became a good friend. She kept her promise: I was busy speaking at high schools. She wanted everyone to share in the experience of hearing my presentation. I never could easily mask my emotions. Therefore, anyone who knew me could tell when I was upset, extremely excited, or frustrated over something. And Karen was astute. She had a knack of throwing my own words of wisdom right back at me, "You told me yourself, one time, Sharon, 'Life isn't easy.' What makes you think a divorce is going to be any easier? It's part of life."

"I know life isn't easy, but why does it have to be so doggone difficult sometimes? And lately I've been tested to the max."

"Well, you know what they say, the best thing is to keep working, keep busy. I'll just keep finding you more speaking engagements at the high schools. That'll keep your mind off your problems. Everything will work out in the end. It usually does. Besides, the divorce cannot go on forever. It has to be finalized sooner or later." I knew that she was right, but I hoped it would be sooner instead of later.

One afternoon there was a knock at the door. Very cautiously I hollered, "Who's there?"

A man's voice answered, "It's U.P.S. I have a package for you." I had a quick decision to make. I had a choice, I could trust the man's voice or choose not to. I could always have him give the package to a neighbor next door or I could take it myself. I heard the distinct hum of a U.P.S. truck in front of my house. Then I heard the thud of a package hitting my front door. The signals I was receiving indicated trust was in order...I opened the door to the friendly voice of the U.P.S. driver, "Just sign right here on line twenty-six, here, I'll place your finger there and here's the pen."

My mother had always taken the packages when she was here; apparently he had already learned that I was blind. "Here's your package. It's kind of heavy. Here, let me place it inside for you." Very quickly, he reached inside to drop the package into the front foyer. He never entered my house himself. "Have a nice day, now, and don't forget to lock your door."

He was definitely one of the nice ones, I thought, one of the people who are sensitive and warm and caring. I know they are out there. It's just up to me to find them.

I wondered what was inside the box. It couldn't be something from Wayne. There was no way he would be sending me anything except legal papers. I didn't order anything recently nor was I expecting a package from anyone up North. There was only one way to find out, I thought, as I carried it into the kitchen and placed it on the kitchen table. Carefully I used a knife to cut the tape that bound the two top flaps together. The box was loaded to the top with papers. There were three sections, each containing hundreds of pages. Altogether, it formed one very large stack of papers. My curiosity was getting the better of me. What could they possibly be? I was never a patient person. Since losing my sight I found that patience was a virtue I was going to have to acquire. Soon the children would be home from school and the boys could read me the letter that accompanied the stack of mysterious papers. I sat and waited for those familiar words, "Mom, we're home!" I rushed the boys into the kitchen where the box was sitting, "Quick, read me what this says."

Marc was the one who took the paper first. "Dear Sharon, the appeal on the case the State versus Rossi is now over. I have enclosed for you a copy of the court transcripts from the original trial, and also the four page opinion that was written by the three judges for the appeal. I did not consider it fair that the criminal should receive these free of charge in prison and was rather upset when I heard that you had to pay twenty-five cents a page. I was not supposed to do this, but I did it anyway. It is for that reason I am not signing this letter. I felt you were entitled to hear what went on during the trial and was rather upset when I learned you were unable to sit in the courtroom during the proceedings. Good luck in having these read to you. You are really a gutsy lady and have my utmost admiration. Sincerely yours, a friend."

After reading the letter, quickly, Marc looked in the box, "Wow, look at all these papers! Are they all the trial, Mom? Boy, it must have taken a long time!"

Marc helped me unload the box and he went to the final page, "I can't really tell what the last page is, mom, but it's one thousand something. There's a lot of pages here. Who's ever going to read them all to you?" I sat there with my eyes pointed at Marc, "Mom, really, that's too much, there's no way that I..."

Quickly I interjected, "Marc, don't worry, calm down, it won't be you." I heard Marc breathe a sigh of relief and make a mad dash for the door and then heard him come running back, "Oh, by the way, do you need me for anything else?"

I started replacing the papers in the box, "No, Marc, nothing else right now. Thank you for reading the letter."

Again faith in humanity was restored. Somebody actually took heart and had sent the court transcripts to me. Yes, there were nice people out there. How ideal it would be, how absolutely wonderful to fill your life with loving, caring, wonderful people and eliminate from your life those who use and abuse and take advantage. Why not do that for myself? I chose my friends, and I would control the path that my life would take. No longer did I have to tolerate the negativism of anyone. If someone wanted to be miserable, he or she could find someone else to be miserable with. I wasn't going to be around. It was one thing to talk out problems to overcome them, but something totally different to live them over and over again, to be miserable, frustrated and continuously depressed. If someone really didn't want to help himself or herself solve problems, it meant that he or she enjoyed being miserable—but from now on, that enjoyment would be without me. The last negative element in my life walked out the door when Wayne left. And I wasn't going to let anymore in.

CHAPTER TWELVE

Crime Stoppers

I was sitting at home one afternoon listening to a television soap opera when I heard an announcement for a golf tournament sponsored by Crime Stoppers of Palm Beach County. "If you would like to help Crime Stoppers in any way, call the crime line." The telephone number was given. I recorded the telephone number. The first three digits were given, but the last four were given in the form of T. I. P. S. It took some time for me to figure out exactly which numbers those letters represented. I dialed.

"Crime Stoppers," answered a woman's voice.

"Hello, my name is Sharon Komlos, and I'd like to know how I can get involved with Crime Stoppers. I was listening to television and they said you were having a golf tournament. I don't really want to golf, but how do you get involved?" The young woman gave me the telephone number of the local chairman of the board of directors, Allen Cushman. I memorized and then dialed the number.

"Cushmans', can I help you?"

"Yes, Allen Cushman, please." I was put on hold for only a few seconds.

"Allen, can I help you?"

I detected a slight Southern drawl in the man's kind voice, "Yes, my name is Sharon Komlos, and I understand that Crime Stoppers is having a golf tournament. Now I'm not really calling about the golf tournament, but I notice that you had an appeal for anyone who wants to help Crime Stoppers. I'm totally blind, and I know crime on a firsthand basis. I have been doing motivational speaking for about the past year and have had some success at reaching people. Do you ever have the need for a motivational speaker to assist in raising funds for your program?"

At first he seemed taken back by my comments, I noticed the hesitancy in his voice. "Uh, what exactly qualifies you for being a motivational speaker?"

I proceeded to tell Alan how I had become a victim of crime. I told him about my loss of sight as a result of the crime. Then there was silence on the phone . . . "Well, let me see, I'll give you a call back. Can I have your phone number? Thank you very much for calling."

As I hung up the phone I had a feeling I would never hear from this man again. I had just received the old, "Don't call me, we'll call you" routine. "Well, at least I tried," I said outloud.

Half an hour later the phone rang. "Hello, Sharon?" Again I detected a slight southern drawl in the man's voice; only this time it was filled with more excitement.

"Yes, this is Sharon."

"Sharon, what can we do for you? Oh, by the way, this is Allen Cushman."

"Allen, that's not the reason I called. What can I do for you?"

"We are having a Board meeting later in May. I will come down and pick you up myself if you would agree to come. I would like you to meet the members on the Board. You know, I was rather reluctant when you told me your story. I really wasn't quite sure who I had on the line. One of our secretaries read about you in *Family Circle* magazine and she told me that your story was definitely valid. I am really looking forward to meeting you, and so is the rest of the Board. Let me check the calendar . . . the meeting will be the second Tuesday in May. I'll give you a call on the Monday before the meeting to arrange for the time. Thanks again for calling, Sharon."

I really didn't know very much about the program. I had listened to some of the re-enactments on television. They re-enacted unsolved crimes. The intention of the re-enactment was to jog the memory of anyone who may have seen anything relating to this particular crime. People with information about the crime could call the TIPS line, remain anonymous, and be eligible for a reward of up to $1,000. The local program had started in Palm Beach County in September of 1981. Since it was a non-profit organization, it had to go out to the public for financial support. Allen explained that he, along with the president of the Crime Prevention Officers Association and a few other concerned citizens, went to Albuquerque, New Mexico, where the program had been established in 1976. He explained how the programs were catching on all over the nation. They assisted law enforcement by acting as a clearing house of information obtained through the anonymous TIPS line. Each program in a community chose its own name, but the methods were the same. There were Crime Stoppers, Crime Lines, Silent Witness, and Crime Solvers. There were other benefits of the program such as a general good feeling that people could fight back against crime. The alternative of anonimity was an excellent way of getting people to tell what they knew without risk. With the added incentive of money, the programs were becoming increasingly successful. This program could be excellent for building rapport among the private sector, law enforcement, and the media. Not everyone agreed about everything at the same time, but one thing we all agreed upon was that if we wanted to make our community safer, we had to combat crime and assist law enforcement. Crime Stoppers was a long step in the right direction.

I met with the Board in May and told them my story. Alan advised me later that month that I had been recommended for membership on the Board of Directors. The Board's purpose was to vote on the amount for each tip received on the anonymous TIPS line. Not every tip was worth $1,000. The board needed to vote on each for its individual merits. Recommendations came through the police coordinator in conjunction with the arresting detective. They were voted upon by the full Board. Another purpose of the Board was fund raising. I felt the key was to increase community awareness and involvement. People had to feel that it was their program, that they would benefit. My first presentation for Crime Stoppers was to one of the Rotary clubs in Palm Beach County. I sat next to Allen during the luncheon prior to the presentation. I asked him, "How many other women are present in the room?"

Allen said with a slight bit of laughter in his voice, "I'm seated next to the only one."

Allen started the presentation by telling the organization the circumstances of my call to him, that I was a victim of crime and that I wanted to get involved with Crime Stoppers. He admitted his reluctance to believe my story and need to check it out with a secretary in his office. He then turned the program over to me.

I told the Rotarians that I was a statistic. I also told them I was a concerned citizen, but more than that I was a very concerned mother and a resident of Palm Beach County. I went on to tell them about the incident that took my sight. "We always seem to think that crime is something we read about in the newspapers or hear about in the news on television at six and eleven. I used to be one of those people. How many of you feel that you live in a safe part of the city and that you can never be touched by crime? Did you realize that we are all exposed? Just by virtue of being a human being on the face of this earth, travelling the highways, going shopping, being a home owner or businessman, we are all exposed. Crime doesn't know and doesn't care what you look like, what your name is or who you are in society. It doesn't care whether you are male or female, and it doesn't care where you live. That hand of crime is very non-selective. It can reach out and touch wherever and whomever it pleases. One step that we can take as citizens of the county against crime is to support the local Crime Stoppers organization."

I continued by telling them a little more about the program. The plea for financial support was soft and subtle, but the story of the crime had touched them. Shortly after our presentation, Crime Stoppers received a check for $500 from the Rotary Club with a commitment to continued support.

I enjoyed my new involvement with Crime Stoppers. I was able to attend only one more Board meeting before my summer vacation. We agreed I would rejoin them upon my return in August.

Between speaking to the high schools and speaking for Crime Stoppers, I felt that the vacation would be a fabulous break for the children and for me. I checked with Howard Zeidweig, my attorney, to find out what was going on with the divorce. He told me there was absolutely nothing to worry about, that he was fully capable of handling the whole thing. He was in negotiation with my husband's attorney and from what he could tell, it would be over with quickly. I remember the words of his last conversation before we left, "Don't worry about a thing. The paper-work should be completed by August and I will send everything up to you by Express Mail. The property settlement agreement and everything is taken care of. From the way it looks now, your husband has once again conceded that the custody and the home shall remain with you. It looks like this is finally going to be it. The final papers will be in the mail. All you have to do is sign them and return them to me. You will be a divorced woman by the time you return here in August. Enjoy your vacation. Don't worry about a thing." I trusted Howard. He is a good attorney, but more than that, he is a good person.

My mind was at ease as we boarded the 727 at the West Palm Beach Airport. Chuck assured me that he would keep an eye on the house. He would keep me informed as to what was going on locally and if he felt there was anything that I should know, he would call me at my mother's home. This vacation was going to be a pleasure. The speaking was going well; I was receiving much needed experience as well as exposure; I found a new involvement with the Crime Stoppers Board; and I was really looking forward to working with them upon my return. And there was the assurance from Howard that the divorce should be over at the end of August. Yes, it was going to be a good vacation.

Chuck walked us onto the plane and as I helped the children get adjusted in their seats, Chuck placed their carry-on luggage in the overhead bins. He gave me a kiss on the cheek, a hug and wished me good luck. I heard him quietly leave, but just before exiting the plane, I heard his voice once again. I assumed he was talking to the flight attendant, "Keep an eye out for that blind blond in the bulkhead seat. She's traveling alone and I know for a fact she can get into some trouble. More than that, she's traveling with three kids. Now that can be a handicap!"

I didn't hear any response from the flight attendant. I guess she was in a state of shock. I felt great, relaxed, and very content. It was going to be a good summer. What could possibly go wrong?

CHAPTER THIRTEEN

Summer Romance

As soon as we arrived at my parent's house, my mother took the children in hand. "I'll bet you're all glad to be out of school. You all have grown a little since the last time I saw you. Come on, boys, help me with the bags and we'll go unpack upstairs. Kristin, do you want to come along too?"

I heard Kristin's little voice speak up, "That's okay, boys, I'll take my own bag. Come on, grandma, I'll take that box too, grandma. That's my Strawberry Shortcake and a few other toys. It's okay. I'm a big girl now. I think I can handle it."

I listened to the four of them as they made their way upstairs. I did so much of that now, just listening. I recalled Kristin's voice when it was higher pitched and had more of a baby tone; now my little girl was growing up. She would be starting kindergarten in the Fall—her first real experience with school. Time passed so quickly. Shawn, now eleven, would be entering the sixth grade, middle school. Every parent heard horror stories of drugs and discipline problems at the middle school. He was always so good up until now; I really didn't think that the middle school influence would change him. Marc had just turned ten and would be in the fifth grade. This would be his final year in the elementary school. As my mother told me when I was younger, "Small children, small problems; bigger children, bigger problems."

All I could try to do was keep those lines of communication open, give them all the love and support they needed through these often trying and turbulent years. *"And Wayne wanted to take custody of them. How would he ever be able to handle them? It takes more than sight to raise three children. It takes understanding, patience, love, and communication. It also takes that all-important support. If Wayne couldn't be supportive of me, if he was unable to communicate his feelings, what in the world ever made him think that he would be able to raise three children and be able to communicate and be supportive of them? Well, at least that is over. Once again, he has relinquished the custody to me."* It looked like there would be no custody battle. I remembered Howard's words, "Don't worry, I'll take care of everything."

My mother again appeared and interrupted my thoughts. "Well, how's Chuck?"

"He's just fine, he sends his love and guarantees he will call me in the event of any emergency."

"You know Chuck better than that. He would probably handle the emergency and not tell you until you return to Florida. He wouldn't want you to worry."

"You're probably right, mom. Oh, by the way, is Millie still cutting hair up at the corner?"

"Yes, and I see her every Friday. Do you want to come along next week?"

"My bangs are long, and I know that the ends could use a good trimming, I was going to try to do it myself, but didn't have enough guts."

Mother agreed to make my appointment along with hers before I did something drastic, like cutting my own hair again.

"How is everything proceeding with the divorce?"

"Howard assures me I will be a divorced woman by the end of the summer. He said he will send the papers up Express Mail. I can sign them and have them notarized and then return them to him. He assures me everything is in order this time. I hope."

"How have the children been taking it, really?"

"We all have our moments. But when we do, we usually just talk it through. We have cried together over this whole thing, mom. Believe me, there have been many tears shed over it. The children wanted to know why, and whether they were in some way responsible. I assured them repeatedly that the problem was between their father and me, and they were not in any way responsible for what had happened. I assured them that they still had a father and that he would see them on the weekends. So far, it has been working out all right. I talked to all the teachers at school to advise them of our home situation. So far, everything has been running smoothly. The teachers haven't noticed any changes in school. One more thing, remember back in November when Wayne moved out? Marc at that time was being tested for the gifted program, you know, the enrichment course. It was a little bit late in the year, but the school notified me in January that he was accepted into the program."

"That's right, that's the program that Marc really wanted to get into because his brother was. What did he have to say about it?"

"You know Marc, sometimes I wonder if anything phases him. All he said was, 'I knew it. It was just a matter of time before they recognized it, too.' For the last half of this year, Shawn and Marc were both in the same class, but I wasn't quite sure if that was a good idea. The teachers seemed to think that Marc was a little intimidated by his more flamboyant and outspoken brother."

"I must say, you have weathered the whole thing fairly well. I hope things really start to look up for you. How is the speaking going? Are you still gaining more 'exposure'?"

"Yes, mom. But you don't seem to understand. I need that exposure because along with that is coming much needed experience. I have to know my audiences. I have to know how to play off of them. I can feel when I am reaching them, and I can feel when I am losing them. I really need this time to keep refining the speaking skills. It will all pay off in the end. Besides, I'm doing a lot of good. I can tell when people come up to me and share a part of their own lives. You really cannot put a price tag on that."

I told my mother about speaking at the high schools and then about my newly found program called Crime Stoppers. I know my mother knew I was right, but she couldn't help wondering when I was really going to start earning a living.

I thought it would be nice to talk with Millie again. She usually cut my hair when I came into town. We didn't know each other in high school; we only knew of each other. We graduated in 1967 and that alone gave us an awful lot to talk about every time I came to town.

"Well, look who's back—Miss Florida. How are you doing? How are the children?" One thing I could say for Millie, there was always excitement in her voice. And she never ran out of things to talk about.

"The children are just fine and I'm hanging in there, too. What's new up here?" I knew the answer would be the prelude to a very long conversation. From the time I sat in her chair, Millie filled me in on all the latest local gossip: Who was getting divorced, who was seeing whom, who moved out of the area and who moved back home. "Remember Rich, the little guy with the big teeth? I understand he's living somewhere in Chicago." Millie continued, "Oh, by the way, do you know who was in here the other day? I know it is no one you would guess. Do you remember Ray, Ray D'Eusanio? Remember him? He was a football player. I think he wrestled too. He was also voted Best Looking in our senior class. He was in here the other day. I was doing his hair. And I must say he is still quite a good looking hunk. We were talking about you."

"Me? We didn't even know each other in school."

Again Millie cut in, "Well we didn't know each other in school either. Well, anyhow, he said he read about you in *Family Circle* magazine. I think his mother gave him the story to read. He was interested because he remembered you from school. He remembers you running around in your majorette skirt. I think every guy in school noticed you. Anyhow, he said the next time you come into town to give him a call. Maybe the four of us, that being Ray and you, along with my husband, John, and myself, we could all go out to dinner. How does that sound? Why don't you give him a call? I think he's back at home at his parents' house."

I was stuck in my line of thought, "Me?" I really didn't know this guy. Instantly when I thought of his name, images of an eighteen-year-old, handsome youth appeared: In his wrestling togs, in his football uniform, and in our yearbook peering into a mirror. "Didn't he ever get married to that girl he was dating in high school?"

"No, he never did get married. And I really don't know why. He really seems awfully nice." Millie insisted that I call, but I had to admit, from her description, she didn't have to insist too hard.

"All right, Millie, I'll give him a call and I'll let you know."

During the ride home, my mother and I discussed this young man I never really knew. I knew of him, and I was sure that he knew of me. "You know his parents really don't live that far. I know Tony and Joanne from dad's Booster Club. I'm really surprised that you and Ray never met. You were both so active in school. I don't see how you could've missed each other." I was beginning to wonder the same thing.

"I guess there's no harm in making the phone call. Would you mind watching the children if I do get this thing arranged?"

"I don't see why not, it all seems harmless enough."

First I called Directory Assistance. They had not difficulty locating his parent's telephone number. I felt nervous as though I had all of a sudden returned to the years of high school. But calling a boy for a date was unheard of back then. Times change, and we were fifteen years older. The telephone began to ring. A woman's voice answered, "Hello." I assumed it was his mother.

"May I speak with Ray, please."

"Just a moment." I could hear her place her hand over the mouthpiece and then call his name.

"Hello." I had never heard his voice before. We never spoke to each other in high school but the strong masculine, husky voice did not fit the image of the boy in my memory.

"I know you will never guess who this is so I'm not even going to ask you to try. But let me start from the beginning. I was over at Millie's getting my hair cut and she told me that you were in there the other day and you were talking about me. My name used to be Sharon Patyk."

The tone of his voice changed. It was more mellow and more friendly, "Well, hello, Sharon, how are you? I never thought you would ever call. Yes, were were talking about you. I read the article in *Family Circle* magazine. My mother passed it on to me. And naturally I was interested. After all, we did go to the same high school together even though we didn't know one another."

I guessed that somehow I still expected him to make the date for dinner. I continued with the suggestions from Millie, "Millie also said something about wanting to get together when I arrived in town? Is that still a possibility?"

"Well, sure that's a possibility. When would you like to do it?" He seemed a little surprised by the offer. Somehow I felt that Millie hadn't being totally honest with me. "Well Millie and her husband, John, are going to pick me up to go shopping on Saturday night. Would you like to meet afterwards, say around nine. We can go to that new restaurant down in the valley."

"First I have a family graduation to attend, but nine o'clock sounds just fine. I'll see you there."

Very quickly I decided to call Millie, "Hi, it's me. It's all set."

"You mean you actually got ahold of him? I really didn't expect it to happen that fast, but that's great. When? I'll mark my calendar. All right, I have it written down, Saturday, July 10th, nine o'clock. Don't forget, John and I will be over to pick you up at seven. We're going to go shopping first, just like I promised."

I don't know why I was nervous, but I was. Here I was, thirty-two years old, but I felt like a teenager of sixteen going out on her first date. I think what made it more interesting was that Ray was someone from my past, someone I should have known in high school, but who now fifteen years later I was going to meet for the first time.

Millie and John arrived as promised at seven p.m. We completed our shopping and had no difficulty finding a quiet table at the restaurant. I was getting anxious, and it showed. "Millie, what time is it?"

"Just relax, we still have five minutes."

"How do I look, is my hair all right?"

"You look just fine, Sharon, believe me," interjected Millie's husband,

John.

Again we engaged in some trivial conversation, but again I couldn't help asking, "Millie, what time is it now?"

"Take it easy, it's only nine o'clock. You have plenty of time. So what if he's a little bit late."

"There he is, he's just coming in now. Ray, we're over here."

I heard his now familiar voice, "Hi, Millie, hi John, how are you? I hope you haven't been waiting too long."

I could feel him standing directly to my left. I was too nervous to move or say anything. "Hello, Sharon." I extended my hand and looked upwards towards his voice. But he reached down for my hand not to shake it but to hold it gently and then reached down and gave me a kiss. Needless to say, I was taken aback. He sat down in the vacant chair to my left.

"Well, I'm going to let you all order. I really don't want anything. My cousin's graduation party was about all I could handle, but please feel free to order. I'll join you for drinks."

We engaged in the usual formalities: The children, life in Florida, life in Garfield Heights, local changes, and news of mutual friends. It was pleasant conversation, nothing too strained, nothing too personal, and nothing too heavy. It was a pleasant, "get acquainted" evening.

When it was time to leave, Ray offered to drive me home. "I won't hear of it. We brought Sharon here and it is my responsibility to see that she gets back home safe and sound. Besides, the children would never forgive me if something happened to her."

"Really, Millie, it's all right, I think I would be safe with Ray. It's rather late, and you and John have much further to travel. Ray's parents live only a few streets away from mine and since he offered, I don't think there would be much of a problem."

"Really, there's no problem, Sharon. We brought you here and..." Then Millie hesitated for a second, "Well, all right. Do you think you're going to be okay? It is a little late and I am kind of tired. All right. Ray, you be sure she gets home safe."

"Yes, Millie," Ray said.

We all walked out to the parking lot, only this time I held on to my new partner. I thanked Millie and John for the lovely evening and then leaned over to Millie and whispered to her ear that I would give her a full report in the morning. I knew she would be waiting. Ray helped me into his car.

"I don't think my parents will ever move out of that house," Ray said.

"I don't think mine will ever move, either."

The ride back to my mother's house was brief, too brief. "Would you like to come inside?"

"Aren't you tired?"

"I'm not that tired."

We walked into the living room and over to my mother's couch. All of a sudden, we were two kids in high school. It no longer felt like 1967 instead of 1982. "You have very strong arms, I noticed that. How is the rest of you." I was polite. After all this was a first date, and I didn't want to take any liberties which might make him uncomfortable. I gave him the option of first refusal.

"I guess there's only one way for you to find out. I don't mind if you don't."

I placed my hands on his shoulders and then ran them down both of his arms. His shoulders were broad. His chest was muscular and strong. "Millie was right, you really did maintain your physique." He just laughed a little at my observation, "And what else did Millie tell you about me?"

"She just said you are as handsome today as you were fifteen years ago. Well, maybe just a little older, but according to her the years have really been kind."

"You look very nice as well. Millie said you had changed, but she didn't exactly say how much. I recognized you from the picture in *Family Circle* magazine and from seeing you on the morning talk shows. The years have been kind to you as well." I admitted that I had changed since high school and was thankful that I had.

The conversation then turned to my children. I told him about my two boys and little Kristin. "Kristin will be starting kindergarten this Fall. It will be so nice to have the whole day free."

Ray admitted that at one time, when he was younger, he would have liked to have married and had a family of his own. But now, no way, "You won't find me pushing a baby carriage around, I'm just too old for that."

"You mean you don't like children?"

"I think children are just fine, as long as they're someone else's."

I decided it was best not to continue the conversation about the children. "And what are you going to do with all that spare time when your daughter starts kindergarten?"

I told Ray about my speaking and my new involvement with Crime Stoppers. I explained a little bit about the program. I told him that the speaking was finally taking shape and I enjoyed what I was doing. My hopes for the future were to continue to speak and reach people who felt they could not overcome adversity in their own lives.

"Why didn't you ever get married? Weren't you dating the same girl all through high school?" I did not feel I was treading on forbidden territory. I felt he had been asked this question more than once.

"I just never found anyone with whom I wanted to spend the rest of my life. I have seen too many of my friends get married, then divorced. I've also seen the worst side of marriage. I've seen the unhappiness, the arguing, the fighting, and the cheating. There are just too many times that I've been sworn to secrecy not to tell about a wife or a husband who had been cheating. I'm perfectly content being alone. Now I'm not saying I don't date, because I do. And I have gotten serious over a woman more than once. But never serious enough to get married. Now let me ask you one. Millie already told me that you are getting divorced. Is it final yet? Do you think it was because of what happened?"

I really liked his point blank questions; there's no beating around the bush with this man. "No, the divorce is not final yet, but my attorney guarantees me that I will be divorced by the end of the summer. He really seems to think that everything can be resolved by then. And as for why it happened, it is really difficult to say. I don't want you to think I'm avoiding the question, but sometimes I really don't know. Time seems to distort reality and as more time passes, I begin to wonder exactly when the loving stopped and when the complacency took over. All I know is that after the shooting I had the feeling that my husband thought he had really lost something he would never find again. He even admitted that he never realized how much he really needed me. I wonder how long our marriage was based on that much need and so little love. It steadily declined from that point until we went to an in-house separation. That was May of last year. The situation became more impossible and finally so unbearable that Wayne moved out in November. The more I think about it, the more that I feel I have been divorced for a long time, much longer than I first realized. Like I said, reality has a way of getting distorted with time. Too often we make ourselves believe things that were never there to begin with and, on the other hand, we sometimes make up our own little stories to cover up for the inadequacies that were really there. All I know is what's happening now. I am getting divorced and as far as I know I am getting custody of the children."

He seemed to appreciate my honesty. "That just goes to prove my theory. That marriage certificate, the piece of paper that two people sign before they get married does not guarantee that somebody is going to stay with you forever. It doesn't guarantee that two people will stay in love forever. Too often it can be a false sense of security."

"My goodness, you sound so cynical over marriage. You talk as if you don't even believe in it at all."

"Don't get me wrong, I think marriage is a great institution, as the old phrase goes. And it's wonderful if two people can fall in love and stay in love, but as of yet, I just haven't found that person. I'm not adverse to marriage, let's just say I'm cautious and I tread softly. Everything just has to be right."

He put his arm around my shoulders and bent over and kissed me on the cheek, "It's getting awfully late. You look like you're getting tired. I'm sure your children will be getting you up bright and early tomorrow morning."

"I won't be leaving until August, maybe we can get together again, one more time, before I leave."

His response came quickly, "When?"

"Next week?"

"Fine, any day but Monday is good for me."

I thought for a moment, "How about Wednesday or Thursday?"

"I'll see you again, Wednesday night."

I walked Ray to the back door and once again was thrown back to high school days: Saying good-bye to my date at my mother's back door, quietly closing the door to the kitchen for one last good night kiss. Today was no different. One good night kiss led to another, then another, and another. I really didn't want them to end. They were soft, gentle and tender. We both knew they would have to end. Finally we said good night and I locked the door behind him. I listened to his footsteps as he walked down my mother's driveway. I heard him open his car door and slam it shut. I listened for the sound of his car starting and then leaving. I walked into my bedroom and started to get ready for bed. I thought about Ray for the rest of the night. His arms were strong, yet he was so tender. He was very straightforward and was filled with cold reality. But there was a deeper, more sensitive, compassionate side to this man I wanted to know. It didn't seem to matter that I didn't know him before. I had locked in my memory that strong and handsome eighteen year old. Ray was fifteen years older now; to me he hadn't changed. Millie was right, he was still strong, and I definitely believed her when she said he was still handsome. I wondered what my children would say if they were to meet him. Equally as important, how he would feel meeting them?

The weekend had turned into the weekdays and Monday morning

brought business with it. I received a phone call from the local morning talk show asking if I would be able to do another interview while I was in town. It was scheduled for Thursday morning. Some of the towns-people also wanted to hear me speak, so they scheduled a talk at one of the local churches. That date was set for the first week of August. I tried to keep myself as busy as possible so that Wednesday would come more quickly. I decided to brief the children about Ray before my date with him on Wednesday night. I went upstairs and found my old yearbook and brought it downstairs to the children.

"Come over here for a second, kids, I want to show you something." I handed the yearbook to Shawn as they all gathered around. "This is my old high school yearbook..."

Shawn interrupted, "1967!" They started laughing and Marc broke in, "Mom, that was in the old days, wasn't it?"

Very quickly they started flipping through the pages. "Mom, look at the funny clothes. Did people really wear their hair like that?" Shawn asked.

"All right, let's just take it easy. Look for my name, I wasn't married back then so it would be the same as grandma's, Patyk, P-a-t-y-k." I heard Kristin start giggling, "That's you, mom? Look at your hair!"

I remembered the picture in the yearbook. My hair was short cropped and curly, but I still had my bangs. I was really nothing much to look at. My mother quickly came in offering assistance, "Here, I'll show you where your mother was a majorette. And in this page she was queen's attendant. And then over here is where she was in the school variety show."

My mother went on and on showing the children all of my pictures. Then I broke in. "Do you remember the man I was telling you about, the man from the other evening who I met when I went out with Millie and her husband John? Look under the last name D'Eusanio, D'E-u-s-a-n-i-o."

"Is his first name Ray, Mom?" Shawn asked.

"That's him," said Marc.

I waited for some sort of response, "Well?" How does he look?"

Kristen was the first to speak up, "He's kind of cute, Mom, but it's too hard to tell, because you don't look the same like you do now. I really won't be able to tell until I see him in person." That was a cautious answer if I ever heard one, it was very diplomatic, even from a five year old.

My mother then proceeded to show the other pictures of Ray, "Here he is again under King's Attendant, and here is his wrestling picture with the varsity wrestling team. And he's somewhere over here in the football team, too."

Just then there was a knock at the front door. "I'll get it," said Shawn. First he peeked out the window, "I think it's him. It sort of looks like him. Hi, my name is Shawn, you must be Ray. Mom's been waiting for you." Nothing like the honesty of my own children, I thought.

"I was just showing them our old yearbook. I wanted their own opinions as to how gracefully you really aged."

I could feel Kristin's probing eyes checking him out. Quietly but rather obviously, she wandered over and whispered in my ear, "Don't worry, mom, he's still handsome." I laughed at my daughter's observation. I continued with the introductions, "Well, Ray, you already met Shawn. Over here, somewhere, is my son, Marc, and this is Kristin. Children, this is Ray."

I breathed a sigh of relief. They were all now formally introduced. Kristin stayed close to me, cautiously checking out this stranger for herself. I had to give my last words of motherly instructions to my children, "All right, now. Please, do not give your grandmother a hard time. All right? And Kristin, remember, bedtime is no later than nine o'clock. You know that goes for you boys, also. Right?"

Our date went smoothly. We decided to go dancing, and I promised to dance fast only if Ray would not leave me stranded on the dance floor. I enjoyed the slow dances. I had danced with men before at various functions in Florida. But this was different. It felt wonderful to have his strong arms wrapped around me. It had been a long time since I had felt such tenderness.

This date was the first of many to follow. Ray watched my television broadcast on the morning talk show, and he offered to drive me to my next speaking engagement. He offered to accompany me on two radio interviews that had been booked during my visit to Ohio. I just could not believe this man; he was absolutely wonderful. I had, however, one reservation which could put an immediate halt to our growing relationship: The children.

Ray got along beautifully with the children, and they took to him immediately. We had a couple of good outtings before I asked him about the subject of children. I understood that he did not want children. I really had a difficult time understanding this since he really got along so well with them. I remember him playing with Kristin at the picnic. She didn't take to just anyone. I listened to them laughing and talking as he pushed her on the swing and the boys as they played baseball together.

We had been up front and honest with each other so far, so before our relationship went any further, I wanted to know why he did not want any children.

"I never said I didn't like children, I just said I didn't want any of my own. I told you before, you wouldn't catch me pushing any baby buggies. I love kids. I have two nieces and three nephews. And I love playing with them. I also enjoy playing with your children. But starting all over again from the very beginning? That is something that I don't want. I like children like yours: they're already here. They're people. You can talk to them, and reason with them, at least, most of the time."

I could now breathe a sigh of relief. At least I felt comfort in knowing that the children would not pose any problems. "By the way, my sister, Donna, is having a birthday party for my niece, Erin. She's going to be one year old the end of the month. Do you think you and the children would like to come to the birthday party? It would be a good opportunity for you to meet the rest of my family."

"I know we would love to."

"You are seeing an awful lot of Ray, don't you think?" my mother asked when I told her.

"Yes, I guess I have been."

"Don't you think it's a little bit too soon, your divorce papers haven't even been signed yet."

"Don't worry, Mom, it really is nothing serious. I'm going to be leaving in August, remember?"

"I just don't want to see you get hurt again."

I thought about what my mother had said, not moving too fast, being vulnerable. These words were not really spoken yet they were implied. And I could really understand her feelings. She just did not want to see me get hurt again. I wondered, what was too fast, and just how long did one have to know a person before really falling in love? Were there time frames by which to gauge a relationship? Everything just seemed so right. Ray liked the children and the children liked him. His family was very nice and the children could not have enjoyed themselves more at the birthday party. Ray was a man of few words, but those were honest and true and backed up one hundred percent by his actions. Time was running short, the summer was ending. It was going to be extra difficult leaving Cleveland this time.

Ray took as great an interest in my speaking as in the children. He handled two radio interviews like a trooper, and then came to a speaking engagement. He had never heard me speak before, and I had to admit that I was a little bit nervous just knowing that he was in the audience. What really happened the night of the attack had never been discussed between the two of us. I knew he had read about it in *Family Circle* and had heard it only briefly addressed on the television and radio interviews. This was different. He led me up to the lectern and placed the microphone in my hand as if he had done it many times before. I started my normal presentation, briefly introducing myself and going right into the attack that had left me blind. I continued with the attitudes of other people, and the expectations they had for me. I told them about the Division of Blind Services and the treatment I received. I continued on about the syndromes that most people fall into when faced with adversity, the world of "what if's," and "why me's." I then turned to the more humorous part of the talk, my children. I recreated a few of our own little obstacles that needed to be overcome. I spoke about the shopping trip to the local grocery store, and how the children could take advantage of me, and did. I mentioned that it was actually possible for me to leave a grocery store, or any crowded place, with the wrong children. I closed with my thoughts about the past, the present and the future. There was a standing ovation and then a few questions.

After the presentation, Ray walked up to the lectern, took the microphone and placed it back on the stand. He led me back to my chair. He stood behind me, quietly, just observing. He stood by and listened; He listened to the questions and the comments expressed by the people as they came up to shake my hand. And then, as the last person passed by, he stepped forward and reached for my arm. Quietly we walked towards the door. It was not until we returned to the car that he said, "You were very good. I really didn't know quite what to expect, although I had some sort of idea from listening to the other interviews. What I found most interesting was the reaction of the people. I sat there watching their faces as you delivered your presentation. You actually had some of them in tears. They were all attentive. I know you couldn't see them, but I know you could feel it in the room. I would think you could feel it from the silence. You actually had them all. There were no bored faces. And then instantly, before they even knew what hit them, they were laughing. I didn't know if you could hear them or not because some of them didn't know if they should or not. But they were, I could vouch for that and I was sure you could feel the laughter, because you hesitated in all the right places. I think you really helped a lot of people in there."

I just sat there listening to his observations. He was so supportive. I leaned over and gave him a kiss on the cheek. "Thank you, Ray. Thank you so much. You have really made this vacation a most enjoyable one, but you realize it's coming to an end a lot quicker than I would like. For the first time since the incident, I am really considering moving back to Ohio."

There was silence in the car as we pulled up in front of my mother's house. "I really don't want to see you leave, either."

Something was being left unsaid and I just couldn't figure out why. Why was it so difficult to express my own feelings. I could only rationalize that it was that fear of rejection, the fear of opening up my heart to another person, and then having him tell me that I read the situation wrong. So better than opening up, I closed up.

"Do you think your divorce will be finalized before you leave?"

"I'm supposed to call my attorney tomorrow morning. He should have the papers by now to be forwarded up to me, here in Ohio. Why?"

"I just wondered." Could it be that there was something that he was holding back as well?

As promised, the divorce papers were sent Express Mail. They were drawn up according to Wayne's specification, as relayed through his attorney. They were sent to Ohio for my signature. My mother read every clause aloud and everything seemed to be in order. I would have custody of the children, receive child support payments, and keep the house. I signed the papers, had them notarized, and returned them by Express the very same day.

We returned home later that afternoon to an emergency telephone call. "Your attorney, Howard, called, Sharon. There seems to be some sort of problem. He said to call him back right away."

I couldn't figure out what went wrong. The papers were here and gone. Wayne had seen them and agreed to them, what could possibly be the urgency for this telephone call.

"May I speak with Mr. Zeidweig, please? Yes, this is Sharon Komlos. Yes, I'll hold. Thank you." My mother sat by impatiently waiting to find out the news.

"Yes, Howard, what is it. Oh, no, really. But why? I thought it would be over. They are already in the return mail. All right, why not? That long? All right, I'll see you when I get back home. Thanks, Howard."

My mother took the phone out of my hand and hung it up. "What's wrong?"

"Howard just told me that the papers we signed will not be good. It seems that now Wayne refuses to sign them, he wants custody of the children again."

In a soft tone my mother asked, "Now what?"

"Howard said we would now have to file for a hearing date. This whole thing will have to be decided by a judge. Howard said he's not going to fool around with any more property settlement agreements. They just don't seem to work with Wayne. The earliest we can get a court date is in January. I can't believe this is happening!"

I thought for sure by now the divorce would have been finalized. It was not easy for me to understand fully what was going on. Somehow, Wayne's decision to go for custody again did not surprise me. When I met with Ray later that evening, I broke the news to him. Now, for sure, I could not even contemplate a move up to Ohio until after January, after the divorce hearing. And even after that, who knew what would happen? I just wanted him to hold me tighter. I didn't want to leave, ever. I told him about the custody battle and that the reason Wayne felt I was unfit was because I could not see the children. "From what I can tell, you have done a very good job with them so far. And if their behavior is an indication of your capabilities, I see no reason why you shouldn't have custody of them."

"Oh, how I just want this whole thing to be over and done with!" I knew he could sense the disappointment in my voice, "Raymond, I think you already know how I feel. I think I'm falling in love with you." I was still being cautious, still not wanting to expose myself even though I thought he felt the same. Not until I heard those words from him would I relinquish all of myself.

"You know, Sharon, I really enjoyed all of the time we have spent together. I think your children are absolutely fantastic. I wish there was something I could do for you to ease the pain. When we met, I really wasn't looking for anyone. A steady relationship was the last thing I had on my mind. But you caught me when I wasn't even looking. I think you already know how I feel, but I'm going to say it. I love you, I really do. And I really hate to see you leave. I've learned from experience that long-distance relationships just don't work out. I know you can't stay up here."

Before he even had a chance to finish what he was going to say, I found myself making an offer, "If you ever should want to come down to Florida, you know the children and I would love to have you."

"You never know, I may just take you up on that offer."

Saying good-bye is never easy, but this time it was extra hard. When my mother and father took us to the airport, there was one more person going along: Ray. We both vowed to keep in touch, but somehow it was just not enough.

"That offer still holds. Anytime you want. Just call us and you know we will be waiting."

While walking into the plane holding onto Ray's arm, I tried to pry my thoughts away from us. I tried to think of all the things I had to do once I returned home. Prepare for the divorce. That was priority number one. The speaking, I already had a couple of high schools lined up for the fall. And then there was Crime Stoppers. I was quite sure, at least I hoped, they would be able to keep me busy. But all the thinking dissolved as he leaned over, gave me a final kiss and said good-bye.

Chuck was there, as expected, waiting to drive us home and hear all the details about our summer vacation. The children filled him in about Ray and Erin and Dawn, Ryan, Mark and Angelo, his nieces and nephews. All of these names were new to Chuck. I continued where the children ended. I told Chuck about Ray, and about the summer.

School started, and I had the full day to myself. I occupied my time with a thorough house cleaning. There were lengthy telephone calls to Mom and Ray. We had both thought long and hard about our relationship. He also thought about my offer. We both knew it was impossible to carry on the relationship long distance until after January. We wanted to be together and there was absolutely no reason why we shouldn't be. Why did we have to wait? I had put my life on hold long enough for Wayne, and it seemed as thought I was doing it again. Why should I let him control me any more? Ray insisted I check with my attorney before he made a final decision to move down to Florida. I talked it over with Howard, stressing my own feelings and reasons for wanting Ray to be with me. Mainly, we were both in love and wanted to be together. I saw no reason to hold off any longer, to await the final decree. As far as I was concerned, the marriage was over a long time ago. The only things left were the formalities. Howard admitted he had no idea how long those formalities would take. Ray decided he was willing to take the risk. The only one way we were going to find out if our relationship would really work was if he came to Florida and spent twenty-four hours a day, every day, with a blind woman and her three children.

On the morning of September 22nd, 1982 I received my much awaited phone call, "I'm on my way." Even the children were excited. They liked Ray, and I knew he would be a wonderful influence on them. I knew the children were curious, and it was Marc who verbalized what he was thinking.

"Mom, are you and Ray going to get married?"

"I really don't know, Marc. That's why he is moving down here. I really don't think it would be fair to me, to Ray or to you children to make the decision right now. First, we have to wait for the divorce to be final. Then, we are just going to have to wait and see how everybody gets along. Don't forget, Ray has never spent twenty-four hours with children. He has never been with you when you had to do your homework, when you were sick, or when Kristin argued about her bedtime. It isn't going to be easy. Everybody is going to have to make adjustments. But at least we are going to give it a chance."

The whole thing really seemed to make good sense. Even Marc agreed.

It was about 5:30 in the evening on September 23rd, when Kristin yelled, "Mommy, he's here!" Those were the words I had awaited.

"We're going to see if he needs any help," Shawn yelled halfway out the door.

I turned around, reaching for the dishtowel to dry my hands. I turned for the door. Before I took a step, I felt his presence in front of me. And then, without any hesitation, I found myself in his familiar arms. He was not bashful or shy in front of the children. A long, hard, wonderful, passionate kiss was in order, just like it was supposed to be. We were two people in love, willing to take a risk and go for it in spite of adversity.

The divorce became final on February 14, 1983, Valentine's Day. A judge decided the major issues. The house as the "primary physical residency" of the children remained with me. All the negatives which began with that night in May 1980 had now played themselves out. There were no remaining obstacles to my achievement. It was now all up to me.

I could always look back at the past and ask myself all those "What if?" questions. So, what if I had not moved to Florida? What if I had not been traveling alone that night? What if I had not suffered the attack that took my sight? Looking back did not change what happened. Instead, I have kept my thoughts on the present and the future. What happened cannot be changed. I have met some wonderful people and have found a new profession. I am now giving of myself and helping others overcome their problems. I have also found someone with whom I can share my life. And I have found that if you give enough of yourself, offer love and compassion to all those who need it, the good will come back to you over and over.